LOVE ACROSS BORDERS

OPPORTUNITIES AND OBSTACLES
FOR EXPORT BRIDES

ELLETTHA
SCHOUSTRA

PublishAmerica
Baltimore

First printing

Softcover 9781627729819
PUBLISHED BY PUBLISHAMERICA, LLLP
www.publishamerica.com
Baltimore

Printed in the United States of America

Contents

PART III

AVOIDING PROBLEMS

Foreword

Opinions differ about the meaning of a harmonious married life, as every culture has its own traditions and ideals. In the Western world, we see the stability of marital relations decreases. At the same time, the institution of marriage not only seems to be more popular than ever but also grows in versatility. E.g., in the Netherlands, traditional marriages are complemented by so—called civil partnerships and legalization of gay marriages.

Moreover there is a spectacular increase in intercultural relations. But this increase is not entirely successful, which has a negative effect on the tolerance of these relationships.

As a social anthropologist, I lived in and traveled through Arab, Asian and other African countries for business as well as private purposes. I met with mixed married couples, a local husband with a wife from a West European or North American country. From conversations with these women I learned that they often felt pushed to the limit to meet the expectations of their new families. However, it was not the family who was pushy, the women posed these demands on themselves as the communication with spouses and in-laws did not go smoothly. Whether the mutual attitude was a critical or a cordial one, it always was difficult to grasp what the other party meant. Quite a few of these women felt so frustrated by the feelings of confusion and uncertainty that the marriage did not survive, even if direct marital conflicts were absent.

Why do intercultural relationships after a bright start so often end in the ditch? What are the causes of the high divorce rates? What can be done to improve the situation?

These questions concerned me and I decided to do further research. During my study period at Leyden University much attention was paid to family systems. Patriarchy, matriarchy, role and obligations of parents and spouses, custody of grandparents on grandchildren, loyalty between family members, differences in rights and duties between men and women, rules of conduct between blood relatives, solving internal conflicts, all these subjects I followed with great interest. Reason enough for further study on a new aspect of this subject, the fortunes of intercultural marriage relationships.

This book is primarily aimed at young Western women who enter into a marriage with a foreigner and settle in the husband's country. In particular when the foreign man comes from a culture where family life, perception of religion, norms and values are different from her Western country.

The basis of a good family relationship is in principle the same in all cultures. Love, mutual support, protection of the weak and vulnerable members, tolerance and loyalty, welfare and harmony are based on these principles everywhere. But that does not mean that the implementing of these principles are the same everywhere. Rather, the reality of a harmonious family life differs from culture to culture. The confrontation with the family life of her husband is often a culture shock for the foreign bride.

This book aims to be a support for partners of intercultural marriages and their families. Not only they, but also society will benefit by stable intercultural relations.

"East is East and West is West and never the twain shall meet." The time of this well-known quote from 1892 by the English poet Rudyard Kipling lies far behind us. The encounter between East and West runs fiercer than ever. Intercultural marriage and other intercultural relationships are a fact of today.

Ellettha Schoustra

The Hague, Netherlands 2013

Introduction

In world history, there have always been intercultural marriages. In historic times, marriages were arranged between countries to strengthen international relations or ratify peace treaties. These politically motivated marriages have vanished from modern society. However, these days, intercultural relations of a personal nature do flourish. The chances to meet partners from other cultures dramatically increase. Temporary migrations, vacations to exotic destinations, pen friends, international study tours, internships abroad, and - not to be underestimated - the internet, these all seem to offer limitless possibilities.

Are intercultural marriages vulnerable? Each item of cultural difference might be a seed of conflict. Therefore, in an intercultural relationship knowledge and understanding of each other's cultural peculiarities are of vital importance to make it successful. More so, as statistics show that the failure rates of intercultural marriages are significantly higher than in marriages where the partners have a similar cultural background. Why are intercultural relations unstable? Are these differences really that important? Do partners make the same mistakes again and again? Is it a taboo to look at intercultural relations with critical eyes? But more important, what can be done to increase the success rate? This book tries to find answers to these questions.

Information about intercultural relations is readily available. In particular from people who are, or have been, in such a relationship and have written their life stories. Some of these stories led to feature films and documentaries. In these movies the focus is on the emotional side of the relationships and less on practical aspects.

Ego documents

For a long time life stories, biographies and autobiographies of women, who are married to intercultural, or ethnically mixed partners, have been published. It is almost exclusively Western women who are or were married to an exotic partner from another continent, who pick up the pen. Most of these authors experienced a failed marriage. In these so-called ego documents they write about the first meeting with the future husband, their married life in her and in his country, the ups and downs of married life, the divorce and its aftermath. Each author does so in her own way and with different emphases, but all of them mention the extreme situations they were caught up in. Due to the lack of a "control group", these stories cannot be seen as representative for the development of ethnically mixed marriages in general. But although most of the writers are divorced, this does not mean that they look back on their marital period with merely negative feelings. On the contrary, quite a few of them describe this episode as an experience that has enriched their lives.

The authors themselves are not looking for sensation, although some have been accused of showing the culture of their ex-husbands in a bad light. Feature films were made from the books of Betty Mahmoody about her marriage to an Iranian man and of Corinne Hoffman about hers to a Kenyan. Those films, and therefore the books as well, were not well received overall. The criticism not only came from the Iranian and the Kenyan side. Also other Western women who were currently married to foreign men demonstrated against what they called 'sketchy images'.

But although not representative, sensational or commercial, is it worthwhile appreciating the life stories in a different way.

It shows personal courage to write about one's own intimate experiences such as love, suffering, wrong assumptions and naiveté, one's life error, a fairy tale wedding ending up in a nightmare. The authors write to have a dual goal. They want to come to terms with their experiences by writing these down. In addition, they also want to enlighten and support other women who end up in similar situations. Marital problems often lead to feelings of isolation. Peer support in such circumstances can help.

Biographies and autobiographies in particular, are important sources of knowledge for social sciences, history and literature, although the given information is only limited field of study. Whether or not with the help of a ghost writer, the authors tell in their own words how they shape their lives, how they experience reality, why and when they take important decisions. Their migration for marriage sake is a turning point in life in each of these biographies. A migrant faces a quest for a new equilibrium from his or her own identity and place in the new surroundings. The whereabouts of the marriage migrant autobiographies offer a unique perspective about this quest.

The main component of this book is a compilation and an analysis of the information presented in the personal documents to make the experiences and the resulting recommendations more accessible. The contents are not only aimed at women who opt for an intercultural marriage, but also at their support group at home, the parents and friends who can offer an escape route if need arises.

The export bride as a marriage migrant

This book mainly focuses on one category of intercultural marriage. This target group consists of 'Western' women who marry a partner from an 'exotic', non-Western country where a patriarchal family system prevails.

In a patriarchal system, women lack an independent legal position, as they remain under male guardianship for life. The father, husband, son or other male relative is responsible for this guardianship. For women with a Western background who enjoy the same rights as men, this means that they, after marriage, step back in status and independence. Although brought up as fully self-reliant adults, they no longer have the right of self-determination. How these realities reflect in daily life is often vividly written in the biographies. So, the focus is on the combination of Western women with non-Western men. The Western woman is the export bride.

There are good reasons to target on this particular group. These types of marriages require the most adaptation on the part of the Western woman. Besides, a lot of literature and data are available about such relationships.

The situation of the counterpart relationship, a Western man who marries a non-Western woman, is not addressed in this book. The position of such couples is different, even if it is the Western man who follows his partner to her home country as an import bridegroom. In such a case the Western husband not only keeps his "natural" status in family law sense, but even makes a step ahead as in the new country he is granted with the status of head of the marital union.

This title only was repealed from the Dutch family law in 1970. Ever since, the status, rights and (financial) obligations of both spouses are equalized.

Equal rights in marital law are an issue too in familiarizing the non-Western marriage migrant who comes to the Netherlands, the so-called import bride. For her it is a new situation to learn she is not subordinate to her husband and has the same rights but also the same responsibilities. E.g., her income – if any – is counted in the joint household.

So, international marriages between partners of two different Western countries with similar legal and political system fall beyond the scope of this book. Broadly speaking, women and men from these countries have the same rights and obligations. So, women in these marriages experience different living conditions than did the above mentioned export brides. Nevertheless, marrying abroad always leads to stressful situations and requires adjustments. That applies to both partners, although there are always more demands on the immigrating partner. But from a legal point of view, the relationship between partners from two Western countries is on a more equal footing. The couple will be able to live an independent life as a nuclear family without special obligations to third parties, such as the in-laws.

The structure of the book

After the Introduction, the first chapter lists the cultural differences between marriage partners and the influence of each of these differences in a marital relationship. Chapter two outlines the differences in family law with its consequences in daily life between modern Western societies and the modern-patriarchal, male-dominated ones. These differences have important implications for the internal responsibilities in a family. In a Western, individualistic society, the care for one's own nuclear family is the first and often the only responsibility of a couple. However, in a patriarchal family structure there are other family members to be considered as well. The well-being of the parents of the husband often comes first. In the third chapter the Western brides have the floor. The export brides tell about the first impressions, adaptation phases and culture shocks that they experienced in their new homelands and how they met these challenges. The fourth chapter discusses other sticking points of everyday life.

The fifth chapter is devoted to family law. Since Napoleonic times, 200 years ago, the legal development of family law has seen tremendous changes in European and other Western societies. In earlier days the power in the family was awarded to the husband, father, or other male guardian. Equal rights of spouses are a recent phenomenon.

The sixth chapter is devoted to the relatives of the bride-to-be. In the first place to her parents, who can support their daughter in various stages before, during and after taking her decision to marry. But also to other relatives and friends, who can provide support. The seventh and last chapter focuses on the bride. With survival tips on how to sustain the challenges of an intercultural marriage, and alarms designed to alert a bride to traps.

One conclusion can be drawn in advance. Partners in an ethnically mixed relationship must be "more able", take more precautions and preparations, than partners in a homogamous marriage. Don't cover up differences or avoid talking about different opinions, but discuss these beforehand. There are consequences for your future life. Chapter 1.2 contains a checklist of mixogamy factors. This checklist can be a tool for a clearer picture of the differences and similarities in a future or already existing relationship. Did the partners learn each other's language, did both of their families approve of their relationship, and is a solid marriage contract concluded?

Well begun is half done. A solid preparation increases the chance of a happy relationship. If so, all involved will benefit. Divorce troubles, especially those with an international character, go hand in hand with heavy emotional suffering and with high costs. The authors of the life stories experienced this all firsthand. Eventually, ethnical mixed marriages will no longer be seen as 'mixed' or 'special'. But before that time comes, there is still a long way to go, a way paved with mixed and special preparations and negotiations.

PART I

INTERCULTURAL RELATIONS

1 Marry across the border

1.1 Introduction

Intercultural marriages have many faces. Bicultural entails the integration of two cultures. Ethnically mixed refers to a combination of different ethnic origins. In relationship terminology, *heterogamy* means "mixed", a marriage between partners of a different social background, e.g. faith or race. 'Mixed blood' is the designation for children born out of "mixed" marriages. The term heterogamy indicates the differences of the social backgrounds of the partners, while the term *homogamy* means that partners come from similar, unmixed, social backgrounds.

Marriages between partners of the two different sexes are identified as *heterosexual*, unions between same sex partners as *homosexual*. Both heterosexual as homosexual couples can be heterogamous as well as homogamous. *Monogamy* is the form of marriage with one partner; *polygamy* is the term for a marital union with more than one partner. Polygamy is divided into *polygyny* (one man with more women) and *polyandry* (one women with more men, this is highly unusual). The degree of mix is called *mixogamy*. Most common worldwide is the marital form that is heterosexual, monogamous and homogamous.

This book mainly deals with marital unions of a heterosexual (male to female) and heterogamous (different social backgrounds) nature.

In the English literature are several more definitions to be found, like: 'Mixed or cross-cultural marriages are taken here to mean marriages between two people from different linguistic, religious, or ethnic groups or nations.'

1.2 Heterogamy and "incompatible time bombs"

According to the general opinion a mixed marriage is a marriage where both partners differ in faith, or racial or ethnic group. But the term heterogamy, the social differences between partners, contains many more criteria. Each of these carries the potential of an "incompatible time bomb," an irreconcilable difference.

To mention a few:

- Nationality. Contains difference in customs, habits and family laws, affects the (in) accessibility of a country, and affects free traffic between countries.
- Long Distance Relationship. Partners are separated at great distances from each other for long periods of time.
- Race or ethnic group. Shows difference in outer appearance, skin color and physiognomy.
- Religion. Difference in faith and religious values has an impact on family law.
- Native language. Has an impact on communication, causes misunderstandings.
- Level of education. May cause problems for mutual communication and understanding.

- Social class. A misalliance, a marriage where partners hail from different social classes, might have legal consequences e.g. in case of inheritance.

- Generation. A large age difference leads to inequality in the relationship and influences the mutual balance of power.

- Marital status. It makes a difference whether the partners before entering into marriage have been married before (widowed or divorced), or that the man is (and remains) already married. In the latter case the new marriage is a polygamous one.

- View on gender. This indicates conceptions on male / female roles in marriage and in society, on 'correct' social relationships between men and women in unequal positions.

- Symmetry in marital choices. Whether or not it is accepted that men as well as women can look for partners out of another group. This criterion is closely related to views on gender.

- Romantic expectations. High romantic expectations or expectations other than romantic ones for future life.

These points require elaboration.

1.3 Data on mixed relationships

Nationality

Nationality as a factor increases in importance. For foreigners from poor countries obtaining citizenship of a Western country by means of a 'passport marriage' is an attractive option. Although immigration laws are getting tighter, it is unrealistic to expect that marriages of convenience will decrease. Arranging such marriages is big business in which a lot of money is involved.

There may be two nationalities in one marital union, or one partner holds dual nationality. The consequences can be either beneficial or dramatic. Two nationalities in one marriage mean that the couple is subjected to two separate legal positions, one in his and one in her homeland. Quite a few women write about this.

The American Betty Mahmoody tells how in Iran, the homeland of her husband, she falls under a legislation which is restrictive for her. Not only is it impossible for her to travel abroad without his permission, but he also has the authority to expel her. He wishes to do so, but wants to keep their daughter with him in Iran. Betty manages to flee from the country with the girl, an illegal action in Iranian law.

The German Ilse Achilles is deported from Pakistan by her Pakistani husband against her will. Their daughters remain with their father who blocks all contact with their mother till the girls are of age.

The British sisters Muhsen are secretly married off by their Yemeni father, under the pretext of going on a Yemeni family visit. Although the father abuses his rights by marrying off underage daughters against their will and without the permission of their British mother, no legal action is taken against him.

Long distance relationship

If a marriage is concluded without a residence permit of the new country for the 'foreign' partner the couple must choose between two evils: either a long distance relationship, or illegal status. A long distance relationship is expensive and uncomfortable, but also allows time to reconsider the option to choose each other. Stine Jensen shuttled for a few years between her home in the Netherlands and her Turkish boyfriend. Eventually she decided not to continue the relationship.

The highly educated philosopher and writer / journalist Stine Jensen, on a holiday in Cappadocia in Turkey, falls for the charms of the Turkish barber Ozan. Ozan styles the actors of a film company. He's never been out of Turkey and speaks no foreign languages. Stine wonders how it is possible that an educated woman like herself can fall in love with a man who is not her equal in this respect. That is "dating down". But the feeling is there. Stine decides to look at her own feelings with an objective view. She reports how it is for a European woman to be in love with a Turkish man. After three years she feels she does not want to marry him, she "leaves in tears'.

Source: Stine Jensen, *Turkish butterflies. Love between two cultures.* Amsterdam: Prometheus 2005

It is no comfortable position for a spouse to live without a residence permit. As an illegal one has no rights, cannot be insured or legally find work. But it is not unusual for a foreign bride to have a shadowy residence status. Often she is insufficiently aware of the consequences.

Race or ethnic group

The factor of race or ethnic group is mainly related to skin color and other physical characteristics. Those features are permanent, white remains white, black remains black. Such a difference can only be accepted, as there is nothing to be done about it. It is noticed, however, that the concept of what is mixed, shifts. Difference in skin color is less often seen as a problem factor.

Religion

Difference in religion is usually such an important factor that it requires active reflection and adaptation of the couple. This will be discussed later. In Islamic countries, the patriarchal family laws are incorporated in religious laws. The confession of a faith is not a personal matter, but a consequence of citizenship. How does a daughter-in-law with another faith deal with this?

Native language

Problems caused by differences in native language often are underestimated. Words can be translated, but to understand the meaning of the special peculiarities of expressions is another matter. In case the couple lives in the country where the language of one of them is the local one, then the partner of the dominant tongue often does not bother to acquaint him/ herself with the native language of the immigrating spouse. Children raised that way miss an opportunity to feel at home in two cultures.

It is no easy start for a bride if she is confronted with a new country, a new family and a new, still unknown language, all at the same time.

Educational standard

Consequences of a difference in education are often neglected, but these often lead to a skewed balance of power in the relationship. A patriarchal man is jealous (or uncomfortable?) with a partner, who has a higher education and earns more than he does. He cannot perform his role as 'guardian' and 'provider' in a proper way, and thinks he is blamed for this. If he tries to control his wife too severely, as compensation to his hurt feelings, the marriage will not survive. Authors Corinne Hofmann and Mirjam van Roode, who married Kenyan husbands, met these problems. However, their love for Kenya as a country remained.

A Ghanaian proverb says: "If a woman, who is too smart, marries, she will not succeed [in her marriage].

Age Difference

An age difference as large as a generation between partners is rarely beneficial, even if this is a conscious choice. According to the so-called "asymmetry hypothesis", this is called: heterogamy in age. Chances of success are even smaller if the woman is the older partner. But these relations do occur. It is often older women, many already grandmothers, on vacation, who then fall for the charms of young men who work in the tourist industry, e.g. in an African country. These women respond to requests for financial support from their partner for sick relatives or to set up a business. Generally, the

women know that they are used by men who will never offer
them a steady relationship with a future. But they appreciate
the - sexual –attention and are willing to bear the costly
consequences.

Social class

How a difference in social class becomes a misalliance is
not always easy to interpret. A misalliance occurs when there
are legal consequences for the 'lesser' party and the children
of the couple, e.g, exclusion of inheritance. But intermarriage
with a partner in higher socio-economic position,' hypergamy
in terms of status and phenotype ' has consequences. Breger
and Hill point out that a marriage is not considered as a union
between two individuals but between two families with mutual
commitments. If the partners do not hail from equal social
classes, discord in the relationships between the families may
be the result.

Marital Status

Difference in marital status before (the next) marriage
seems at first sight far-fetched. But is an important factor,
especially for women. There are indications that women,
who have been married before, are freer to make a choice
of their own when entering into a subsequent marriage. In
the Netherlands, a divorced Muslim woman who wants to
remarry a non-Muslim man meets with less resistance than
would be the case in a first marriage. The failure of a first
'unmixed' marriage constitutes the necessary legitimacy of
another, possibly mixed relationship.

For Western women it does not matter much whether an exotic wedding is her first or her subsequent commitment. But there is a difference if the man is polygamous. A Western woman, who marries a polygamist, will meet few peers. Yet there are Western women who choose to do so. They feel part of a large family where the children of the co-wives also are partly theirs. But they must also share their husband's and enjoy little or no privacy.

In 1978 the white Frenchwoman Claude Bergeret marries the African King Francois Njike Pokam from Cameroon. Claude was born in Cameroon as the daughter of a missionary couple. After a broken marriage to a Frenchman in France, she returns to Cameroon to become a teacher at a missionary school. Then she meets her future husband. He is highly polygamous, after her marriage Claude shares her life with some forty co-wives. They have two children. Claude's environment disapproves of her marriage, the missionary school sacks her. When ten years later her husband dies, Claude remains in Cameroon working for development projects. Claude gives a fascinating and valuable description of family life with rights, duties and responsibilities in a polygamous African family.

Source: Claude Njike-Bergeret, *The White Queen*, 1998

The Spanish woman Sonia Sampayo meets her future husband the Senegalese dance master Pap Ndiaye, in Spain during a visit with his Senegalese dance troupe. After that, Sonia attends several dance holidays in Senegal. In 1997 she marries him in Spain. In Senegal, he has two wives and several children, but he did not conceal his polygamous family from her. He spends most of his time with Sonia in Spain where he earns a living giving music lessons. Sonia is kindly received by her co-wives, though there are definitely feelings of jealousy because three ladies have to share one man. Sonia gives valuable insights into the world of African dance and Senegalese family life.

Source: Sonia Sampayo, *The African princess*. Amsterdam: Arena 2009

But it also happens that a husband is not telling the truth when he claims to be divorced or separated. His Western wife then is unexpectedly confronted with a co-wife, who sees her as an intruder.

Gender

The view of gender relates to the asymmetry hypothesis. Inequality of man and woman is contrary to the Dutch and other Western legislation and general attitudes. But in many parts of the world subordination of woman to man is still the rule. A rule perceived as normal by both men and women alike.

According to the Moroccan sociologist Fatima Mernissi, marriage is not a relationship of love, but one of conflict. The man has rights and the woman has duties. A woman may be beaten... The social system condemns couples to conflict as men and women are each other's enemies. Mernissi wonders why in Moroccan society the man is encouraged to play the role of master instead of the role of lover. The only woman whom a man may cherish is his mother.

Not everyone will agree with the cynical vision of the Moroccan sociologist. But her comments about the marriage mentality contain kernels of truth, which should be considered.

Another aspect of bicultural marriages is the granting of an unequal status: the woman is given a certain status through her husband and not vice versa. The Avalanche Foundation (Stichting Lawine, a Dutch organization which promotes the interests of bicultural families) points out that Dutch women, living in the Netherlands, who are married to foreign men, are seen as *wives of foreigners*.

The view of gender not always is a clear-cut factor.

Romantic expectations

In Western societies, it is commonly believed that romantic love is the (only!) basis for a marriage relationship. The decision to get married is left to the partners; their families have a supporting role at best. But this view is at odds with the reality of arranged marriages. In marital arrangements romance is only the final piece: when the marriage is concluded, after the wedding, love and romance are allowed to blossom. Not before that moment.

Partners may have many down-to-earth reasons for an intercultural relationship. But Western women who marry exotic partners don't think that way. On the contrary, the future husband's exotic background adds to their feelings of romance.

On holiday in Kenya, the Swiss woman Corinne Hofmann meets the Masai warrior Lketinga. She falls in love with the exotic Masai. After the holiday is over, she decides to return to him. She sells her thriving fashion boutique in Switzerland and moves to Kenya. The couple gets married; one daughter is born (July 1, 1989). But the relationship deteriorates, Lketinga tries to control her in an excessive manner, he shows himself to be extremely possessive and pathologically jealous over alleged infidelity. When Corinne cannot stand it any longer, she returns with her daughter to Switzerland in October 1990. Her relationship has lasted for about four years.

Yet Corinne's adventurous marriage is the wonderful story of a modern, well-educated European woman seeking romance in Kenya. The rumors about the merciless climate, primitive living conditions, communication problems and impossible legal procedures with corruption and obstruction do not scare her off. She goes for it. Her books provide a lovely description of life in Kenya, how to cope with the problems of everyday life, the struggle with bureaucracy, infatuation and disillusionment.

Apart from the visible and distinct differences in race, nationality, religion and living conditions, there is a huge educational difference between the two of them as well. Lketinga has had no formal schooling, cannot drive a car, has never been in a high-rise office in an elevator, hardly knows the value of money, can barely read, write or count, and lacks understanding of bureaucratic procedures. Conversely, Corinne seems scarcely aware of the rights and duties of a Masai warrior.

She starts a shop, to make a living for the family. For her husband it seems a normal thing that his wife works for the family income, but at the same time he wants to play his role as head of the family and to present himself as the one in charge of the business. Without any commercial insights about profits, investment, or customer sensitivity, he gives his "friends" the articles for free, and obstructs his wife's business.

For family visits to Switzerland - Lketinga never accompanies her - Corinne needs his authorization. He is not generous in this respect. It also takes a lot of trouble to get his permission for their daughter to travel with her mother (suddenly he is aware of bureaucracy). He has already discussed marriage plans for her.

What Corinne really wants is a European-style marriage with an exotic man. But Lketinga wants a Masai-style union. He considers the qualities of his wife as his property.

Corinne writes that she is unable to tolerate his morbid jealousy and distrust of her. But between the lines one can read that Lketinga distrusts himself. He cannot control her. Is he possessive to save face?

Corinne never stops loving the country and its people, she makes many friends. But in the long run, her ethnically mixed marriage does not survive.

Source: Corinne Hofmann, *The White Masai*.

Differences

All these differences come up in the life stories. Some differences cannot be overcome, others do. A difference in skin color remains visible, an age difference remains unchanged, and nothing can be altered about the personal history of the partners before entering into their relationship. But a nationality can be changed, one can switch over to another faith, master a foreign language, catch up with lost education, wrest oneself free from an unshakable considered social class, or adjust beliefs about gender equality.

In ethnically mixed relationships, combinations of the factors of nationality, race, religion, mother tongue and views on gender equality do play a key role, while issues like education, social class, generational difference and marital status are less prominent.

Statistical biases

The Dutch Central Bureau of Statistics (CBS) does not record racial or ethnic background, or religion. However, these data are important for a comparative study of ethnically mixed marriages. But these omissions are not the only biases. When a woman upon entering into a marriage with a foreigner adopts the nationality of her husband, the couple then lives on as "unmixed married'. In case of a divorce, such a couple remains outside the statistics of 'mixed marriages'. Also, couples who marry in the Netherlands but divorce abroad, or Dutch women who after marrying in the Netherlands depart with their foreign husbands to his country, pose a problem for statisticians who try to shed a light on the (in)stability of homogamous and heterogamous marriages.

The criterion 'country of birth' often is used. But as a definition for difference, this not only misleads statisticians, as is shown in the following newspaper article.

On October 7, 2000, a Moroccan man who has killed his wife, also Moroccan, is brought to trial. His marriage was arranged with the prospect of getting him a residence permit. His wife was also born in Morocco but raised in the Netherlands. As the illiterate man feels entirely out of place in the Netherlands, has no job and does not understand his 'western behaving 'wife, the marital problems escalate with fatal consequences.

The article points to the age and cultural differences between the spouses. The murdered woman was much younger and better educated than her husband and had a lifestyle 'as if she was born in the Netherlands'. The marriage was certainly 'mixed', but in the CBS statistics classified as unmixed because the couple shared the same country of birth.

Source: AD *Haagsche Courant*, October 7, 2000.

There are more examples to prove the unreliability of the 'country of birth' criterion. Suppose that two ethnic Dutch children, who are born on different continents in 'expatriate' families, get married. They settle in their own homeland, the Netherlands. Although fully Dutch by birth, they will be considered (and also treated) as immigrants, as they are 'foreign born'. So, with a bureaucratic stroke of the pen, a new category of citizens is created, 'the statistical immigrants'.

2 Important cultural differences

2.1 Introduction

This chapter starts with an outline of the differences in the social environment between a Western and an Islamic (Arab) society. What happens to women who step from one culture into another? The Arab environment is taken as a default. The Arab-Islamic way of life fully meets the criteria of a patriarchal society, the subject of this book. What is in store for an Arab woman in a Western country? How does a Western woman experience life in an Arab country? What are their patterns of value? What are the facts, and what are the stereotypes?

2.2 Arab woman in the Western World

For an Arab woman, the entrance to a Western European country is a step into another world. How does she cope with the new situation, and what is expected of her? What is strange or striking for our fellow citizens who migrated from Arab countries?

Class differences

In the Western world, class differences are different from those in Arab countries. Although class differences do exist, social mobility through education, occupation, or choice of residence is encouraged. Moreover, boasting about one's ancestry is not considered a virtue. "Achieved status' (achieved by one's own effort) is more important than 'ascribed status' (inherited at birth).

Separate worlds

In the Western hemisphere, socially separated worlds of men and women hardly exist. Co-education in schools is the rule; professional occupations are open to both sexes. The public space, shops, and public buildings are simultaneously used by men and women alike, by day and by night. Shops and offices have no special opening hours or counters for women. In elections men and women line up in the same row in the same polling station to cast their votes. A female compartment in the train, bus, Movie Theater or the church is long gone.

Like in public life, there is hardly any separation in private life. Relatives and friends of both sexes are received in the same rooms by husband and wife together. Husband and wife go out together, social companionship between spouses is important. It is fully normal for male officials, like the postman, streetcar conductor, or plumber to speak to any woman while doing his work.

Although it was only a generation ago that accommodation in youth hostels and camping facilities was strictly separated for unmarried young people, even that is no longer the case.

Legal empowerment for women

Legal empowerment and self-determination for women is obvious, as the ability to cope for oneself is considered important: a woman must be able to live an independent life.

In education, young people are encouraged to think for themselves. By learning to form one's own opinion, which is done by encouraging critical thinking, one can make adult choices later in life. At the age of eighteen, both boys and girls are of age and solely responsible and accountable for their own actions and decisions. Obviously this does not mean that young people stand alone in the world from the age of eighteen onwards. Contacts with family, and care for young adults from their parents continues. But, the change in legal responsibility and authority is alike for both sexes.

(Marital) morality and decency

The double standard in (marital) morality and decency has fallen sharply in recent decades. Adultery as a criminal offence is crossed out of the law. The only legitimate reason left for divorce is "permanent disruption of the relationship." Both partners have the right to file for divorce. Is virginity still a virtue for girls? A girl decides for herself. Macho behavior, trying to get as much sexual experience as possible with girls who do not want the same thing, is seen as annoying and ridiculous. You will not find a young man, who, while being on the prowl himself, at the same time jealously guards his sister against other suitors. Most Dutch people do appreciate the breakdown of the double standard of morality. Good and bad behavior should be equally assessed and valued for both sexes.

But the equality coin has another side too. A woman is less protected. An adult woman is "her own boss", a guardian has no authority any more. The guardian *was* the man who bore responsibility for the welfare of his "pupil", both in private and in public life. But when a girl is of age, she herself is responsible, even if this is difficult for her. Approval or disapproval of her behavior on the part of male family members, who would be eligible for the role of 'guardian', might still be important, but no longer in a legal sense. In the ideal Western world, rights and duties are equally and symmetrically divided. *De jure* and *de facto*, according to the law as well as in daily life.

Patriarchy

An Arabic legal system is usually *patrilineal* and *patriarchal*. This system is an asymmetric one.

Patrilineal means that the line of descent runs along the male side of the family, from father to son. Married men remain members of their own families, married women become in-laws. A married woman has no more obligations to her own family. However, she reserves the right to visit her family and to inherit from them. Besides the clear-cut obligations, there is a range of rules of conduct in family life. The average Westerner fails to notice the subtleties of these rules.

Patriarchal means that the authority of men in family matters is decisive. Within the responsibilities of the "head of the family", the permission for marriages of his daughters and sons is included. Although a mother is actively involved in the partner selection for her children, her final or official consent is not required. A good, caring father negotiates carefully about the marriage contract of his daughter, with the aim of giving her a strong position in her marriage-to-be. A rich, demanding bride has more status with the in-laws than a non-demanding bride without a dowry of her own.

In giving their children properly arranged marriages, parents meet a social and religious obligation. 'To give them marriage' is considered the final piece of the education and the gateway to adulthood.

Women keep male guardians for life. For children, it is the
task of the father, paternal uncle or older brother. For married
women her husband is her guardian, for widows the husband's
brother, or her adult sons. Divorced women do not fit in this
family system. In such a case, her family could be bothered
with the guardianship, but this is seen as an undesirable
situation.

In the Western world, these rules of life usually are poorly
or not at all understood. Many people think that an arranged
marriage is equal to a forced marriage. But these are not
synonymous. A forced marriage (against the wish of one or
both partners) is always arranged indeed, but no marriage is
valid without the proper formalities. Even when the parents
consent to a "love match", correct arrangements are a necessity.
    How this works, is illustrated with the following practical
cases.

In December 1987, the Pakistani politician Benazir Bhutto
gets married. Both bride and groom are 34 years of age.
Benazir has been the leader of the Pakistan People's Party for
a few years already. When her party wins the elections in the
following year, Benazir by then becomes prime minister of
Pakistan. In her autobiography, *Daughter of the East,* Benazir
writes about the press release on her upcoming wedding.
"Conscious of my religious obligations and duty to my family,
I am pleased to proceed with the marriage proposal accepted
by my mother, Begum Nusrat Ali. The impending marriage
will not in any way affect my political commitment. The
people of Pakistan deserve a better, more secure future and I
shall be with them seeking it."

The American magazine *Newsweek* made the following statement about this marriage: "The politician Benazir Bhutto finally bowed to her country's traditions and married the man her mother chose for her."

In response, the author wrote a letter to the editor. "Benazir Bhutto follows her own plans. Had she followed the traditions of her country, then she would have been married off almost twenty years earlier and had stayed entirely outside public life. Now she decides to get married - for reasons of her own- she ensures that the arrangements of her wedding are properly followed. In her case this means that her mother accepts the suit on her behalf."

Newsweek had the commentary included in the letters section.

Source: Benazir Bhutto, *Daughter of the East.* London: Hamish Hamilton 1988

An Indian professor of some forty years of age teaches at an American university. He is a capable teacher, appreciated by his colleagues and students. At a certain time he returns from a holiday in India, and is suddenly married! His parents made the arrangements, and invited him to come to India for this purpose.

The American students are surprised. An adult man with the status of professor has to follow the wish of his aged parents from abroad about the decision whether or not to marry, and with whom?

The Indian professor does not feel embarrassed at all. His wedding was an important event is his family. Although the parents are proud of his professional career, as long as he stays unmarried, their responsibility for his education remains incomplete. Now this final task is done, they can relax and enjoy their old age, which also gives the son peace of mind.

Source: Verbal information

Courtesy

An Arab Muslim woman, who comes to live in a Western country, does not find special facilities for women in public life. She finds no female counter in the post office, the waiting room of the hospital is an "open" space shared by men and women alike, and reserved seats in the bus only serve disabled customers.

If she, in accordance with her own principles, wants to avoid encounters with strange men, she has to be on her guard all the time. The public does not understand her dilemma. In Arab countries, no gentleman will embarrass a lady, but tries to prevent compromising situations for women. There are "safe places" in the public spaces, such as separate waiting rooms at railway stations. A man does not greet a woman in public, gives way to her in a store, coming home, and does not enter the living room unannounced if his wife has visitors.

In certain Western parts of the world, such courtesy is long gone since the feminist movements from the years 1970 -1980. Gentlemen, who graciously offer help to ladies to put on their coats or pull out her a chair, are ungratefully being abused as hypocritical oppressors.

A Muslim woman who leads her life up to standard, dresses properly in long dress and headscarf, avoids encounters with strangers, does not let her children mix with 'strange' other children, prays at the prescribed times, etc., will not be honored in a Western country like she would be in any Muslim country. Correct behavior according to religious rules is considered a personal choice. Any other life style might be valued as well, according to the Western opinion of free choice. However, this opinion of "freedom" is not free, but stressful for a Muslim woman. But the average European is totally unaware of her feelings. On the contrary, more freedom is seen as an essential part of the "liberation" of women. Women of all cultures, that is.

2.3 Western women in Arabia

When a Western woman follows her Arab husband to his country and family, she enters a whole new world.

The Arab in-laws are very friendly and cordial to the foreign daughter-in-law. The family instructs her about proper conduct. The rules are strict, according to Western standards.

There are codes for behavior between men and women, between older and younger generations, and between people of higher and lower class. So, there exists a distinction on three levels. Authority lies at the basis of these relationships. Authority is derived from gender, age, and position in society. Men exercise authority over women; the elderly over young people; and in the workplace, the boss is always right because he is the boss. The relationships are characterized by distance and respect. Familiarity, a critical attitude from young towards older persons or from subordinate to boss is not appreciated. That is rude. Bold directness, like making no disguise of one's feelings, is a sin against courtesy.

The book published in 1971 by the American Marianne Alireza, who in 1943 married her Arab prince Ali Alireza during his study stay in California is still a classic for today's foreign brides in Saudi Arabia. It provides a unique description of Arab family life during the rapid modernization which the country experienced from desert nation to oil giant, just after World War II.

In 1945 the couple leaves for Saudi Arabia with their first-born daughter. The extended family Marianne moves into lives near Jeddah. The Alireza family has a high status and is very wealthy, but their lifestyle is not luxurious and lacks modern amenities. The water for the household is taken from a well in the garden and it is common for traveling Bedouins to make use of the well.

The description of the Arab society of the forties and fifties is very interesting indeed. Marianne recounts the culture shock she experiences when she arrives in Saudi, her awkwardness with the language and customs, her fear and nerves in the new homeland. Everything is new, no one understands her, everything is overwhelming, and the people are very warm, she sometimes feels crushed to death by cordiality, and everything what will happen next is unpredictable. But she also tells how she gets used to her new life and appreciates her family-in-law and the Saudi people and the country. Between the lines, the reader learns much about politics and power relations and practices of Saudi family life. After her famous book Marianne writes more publications on women in Saudi.

In November 2009, in the company of her large offspring, she is interviewed about her life in Jeddah. She describes herself as: "The matriarch of a large and very Saudi family." On January 27, 2010, in Jeddah the ninety-year-old Marianne signs a reprint of her in 1971 published book *At the drop of a veil.*

Source: Marianne Alireza, *At the drop of a veil.* Boston: Houghton Mifflin 1971

Group

Every person is a member of an ascribed group. There is little space for individual choices outside the authority of men. But at the same time, this means that a man, elder person or boss included in one's group, bears responsibility for women, or younger people or his employees. Responsibility can be positive: concern, or negative: control. For a Western woman, who is used to making her own decisions, it is confronting to need spousal approval for activities like an outing to the movies, meeting new friends or to apply for an attractive job. The husband wants to know where she goes, with whom, and why. Suppose she gets entangled in wrong company or otherwise runs into trouble, he is held accountable for the consequences. The society expects him to act like that. A man must make sure that his wife and daughters never impede the 'family honor'.

The social contacts between men and women are strictly regulated, and much more limited than in Western countries. Showing affection in public is not done. No hug upon arrival at the airport, or heading home arm in arm. Spouses usually spend much less time together than in the West. The house, the home is female domain. During the day, men do not stay home but spend their time with other males. Women can visit each other at any hour of the day, announced or not. A man cannot visit another home unannounced. Enjoying an evening together with a snack and a drink on the sofa watching TV is no common practice for married couples. For recreation and relaxation, in Muslim society one seeks the company of one's own sex.

In Arab schools, there is no co-education. In the mosque, men and women pray separately. Women never go alone to public places like parks or beaches; women rarely make use of public spaces and only on strict conditions, according to Western ideas. Enjoy a coffee or ice cream on a sunny terrace? This is only possible within the confines of a club or hotel.

Islam as a lifestyle

According to Muslims, Islam not only is a religion, but a lifestyle as well. Being born as a Muslim means staying a Muslim for life. The civil legislation and statutory interpretation are based on Islam.

In most Western countries, Church and State are separated. Religious precepts and secular laws don't have to be in line with each other. Moreover, one's religion, Christian or other or no religion at all, is considered an individual choice. One can also choose no religion. There is no penalty for not following religious precepts, but a violation of the secular legal system will be prosecuted.

So, within the bounds of the secular legal system, it is possible to live a righteous life without any religious beliefs. A proper lifestyle in Western countries meets social recognition, but this appreciation stands apart from religion. In principle, all religions and lifestyles are of equivalent value. The proper ways in dealing with dissenters are dialogue and communication. But in the Arab-Islamic world, the attitude is different. Moreover, many Muslims believe that a man without a religion is no human being, but is like a dog.

Another point of difference is the identification in passports. Religion, occupation of the holder and his/her father's name are listed in Islamic countries. This is no longer the case in Western countries, to avoid stigmatization. Women as well as men can chose to list the name of the spouse in the passport, this is not mandatory. Every adult person has to apply him/ herself for a passport. In countries with Islamic law this is different; women need the permission of their 'guardian' to apply for a passport. The husband's name is listed in her passport, not her name in his one. The religion is listed as well. For Western wives, it is hard to swallow that the control over her passport, as well as the permission to travel, is in the hands of their husbands or guardians.

Socio-cultural baggage

A Western woman enters Arabia with her own socio-cultural baggage.

For her, the interaction with her husband is characterized by camaraderie without many formalities. If mutual love and respect, the most important characteristics, are established, all other conjugal matters will follow in a natural way, according to common opinion. The relationship is based on mutual equality.

Parents and children go about with each other in an informal way. Parents don't exercise authority just for the sake of it. Parents encourage their children to formulate their own judgments and be assertive. This system works fairly well in the Netherlands. On an average, children stay in the parental home till over twenty years of age, before leaving to live on their own.

In the workplace, a critical discussion with the boss is a fairly normal occurrence. Clarity about the performance of tasks is important for a good work climate. To execute blindly what the boss orders is a bad thing, more so if the subordinate is better aware of bottlenecks in the implementation than the boss himself. The chef also expects his subordinate's critical thinking, to establish a proper job involvement. If women climb in positions of authority, this is accepted.

The society tends towards individualization. Family and friends remain important, but particularly for socializing and emotional support. Not for status. A woman derives her status more and more from her own personality. About the ideal role as a 'wife', there is a social debate. Personal freedom, do what you please, wear what you like, 'feel comfortable'', these things are important for women.

The kinship system in the Netherlands can be characterized as 'double-unilateral'. Both the paternal and the maternal line are equally important in relation to inheritance and other rights and obligations. As parents, father and mother enjoy equal parental authority. The kinship system is symmetrical. That the family name usually comes from the father's side, even if this is no longer mandatory seems to be the last breath of the patrilineal family habits.

The following summary is just an outline of the differences *de jure* and *de facto* between the West and the Arab world women are faced with when they step from one world into the other. Successful marriages take the best of both cultures and adhere less to irreconcilable differences. Being able to do so, one is: 'multiple cultural competent'.

Major differences in marriage and family life of both worlds: Western / secular versus Arabic / oriental / Islamic.

	Western / secular	Arabian / Islam
Love and loyalty	'Love conquers all' if both partners love each other, the basis for marriage is laid and the rest comes naturally.	Love between spouses is nice, but that should arise and grow in marriage. The basis is a proper arrangement.
Role of parents / close family at weddings	Only important for the moral support and acceptance; no formal consent required, from age eighteen onwards every man or woman decides for him/herself.	Formal permission is required, "family council" plays a role in this.
Acceptance of foreign partner by family	Little or no difference in (un) willingness to accept partner for daughter or son.	Accepting foreign daughter-in-law is possible but to accept foreign, non-Muslim son-in-law meets great objections.
Wedding	Official civil registration is the only formality. Church ceremony is a personal choice without legal enforcement.	Registration proceeds following *religious* laws. These differ, according to the religion involved.

Information on marriage contract by government	Usually none, depends on registrar official.	The family must take care of this for themselves.
Legal status of marriage partners	Man and woman equal, symmetry in rights and obligations regarding each other. Spouses owe each other assistance and care, to "provide the necessary".	Husband and wife have different positions, as enshrined in family law. The husband decides, the wife follows. The man cares for his wife and children; the woman is faithful and obedient. The woman cannot be compelled to maintain her husband; she is only the boss on her own money and goods.
Dissolution of marriage	Both parties can apply for divorce, 'guilt' is no argument anymore, permanent disruption is the only lawful reason. In case of disagreement about desire for divorce, usually the applicant's wishes prevail (other party can stop the procedure for a limited period). Court ruling is required.	There is always a question of guilt, judgment is required. Women have limited opportunities to apply for divorce. The husband has this right and he determines the arrangements.

Alternative ways of cohabitation	Many alternatives to cohabitation are socially accepted, gay marriage is legal. No polygamy.	No relationships other than heterosexual marriage are socially accepted. Polygamy and 'Urfa marriages' are included.
Position children	Children of unmarried parents or single mother enjoy the same rights as children out of wedlock. 'Illegitimate children' no longer exist.	Children born outside wedlock are illegal. Such children have fewer rights.
Single motherhood	Unmarried, divorced or widowed mothers receive or hold full legal custody on her child. The (divorced) father or male guardian has less legal authority over the child than the mother.	Mothers do not get legal or parental rights over the child. They may be entitled to care for the child. Judicial intervention is compulsory. A 'male guardian' decides on further education, not the mother.

| Position children after parental divorce | Judge decides about care and guardianship. The standard is either co-parenting, or assignment to one parent (mostly mother) with visitation rights for the other one. Assignment to the father is possible. | Judge or family council decides. Norm: allocation to (family of) the father, visitation rights for the mother is a favor. Mother does have a legal right to care for young children, but this is not always is granted. |
| Alimony | There is a right to alimony, irrespective of which spouse initiates the divorce. | Right to alimony is not obvious. If the wife requests the divorce, alimony is only a favor. |

Participation bride at wedding	Both parties have full public participation; registrar has a duty to ascertain of the free will of both parties.	A marriage contract can be arranged, decided, and closed by the (male) marriage guardian of the bride without her knowledge or consent. The marriage is valid. According to the Koran, to force a bride against her will is forbidden, but it is also true that a daughter must obey her father. The groom is usually more involved in the procedures.
Marriage as a 'rite of passage'	Will be felt as an important step, but otherwise, life goes on as usual (partners already lived together, and women continue to work).	There occur marked changes, especially about the position which the now married woman occupies in the family and in society.

Expectations of marriage	Many, mutually irreconcilable demands. Such as: love relationships vs. individual freedom and equal rights and duties. The relationship is "overloaded".	Rules are clearly defined; both partners have specified roles with rights and obligations. If both of them abide, all goes well.
Inheritance	Spouses inherit from each other, even without a will, special inheritance rights for the surviving spouse.	Inheritance must be defined in a will; non-Muslim spouses often have no right to inheritance of a Muslim husband.

PART II

SENSE AND SENSIBILITY

3 Migration and adaptation

3.1 Introduction

A migration is a challenging, but also a painful process. Both export brides among emigrants, as import brides among immigrants, experience this. Expatriates (expats), employees who work abroad on a temporary basis, have similar culture shock problems with migration stress. Their employers know all too well that the success of the posting abroad depends not only on the expertise of the expatriate worker, but also on proper preparation for the employee and his family. Future diplomats, aid workers, businessmen, missionaries, all those who temporarily leave to work abroad, are offered courses on learning the foreign language, and acquainting themselves with the new living situation, the healthcare and the cultural peculiarities of the new country.

For immigrants in the Netherlands, integration courses with a similar program are offered. But for emigrants, like export brides, such facilities hardly exist, if at all. They are left to their own devices. Nevertheless, export brides are not left in the dark, as there is knowledge available about the adjustment problems of both import brides and expat wives, who often meet similar situations.

3.2 Transition phases in a migration process

The adaptation hassles of import brides are clearly described in *Fortune Seekers* (Gelukszoekers) of Joke van der Zwaard. She distinguishes three main phases:

separation;

transition;

reintegration.

Export brides will also recognize this 'triptych'.

Separation

In the first phase, the period of separation, one has to come to terms with the loss of the familiar old life. But the biographies of export brides often state that the separation period is extremely short, as the relationship becomes a serious one very fast. This happens when for practical or cultural reasons; a free period to experiment with the relationship is reduced to a minimum or is even completely absent. In such a case, a proper saying goodbye to the old life is just skipped. In their haste, a proper farewell to the old life is omitted.

Jacky Trevane is an English woman, who visits Egypt on holiday. There, she falls for the charms of one Omar and marries him within ten days. She does not even inform her family beforehand. But soon it is apparent that she fell in the classic trap of a naive European woman who thinks that "love is enough to overcome everything'. As Omar has no income of his own, the couple must live with his family. Two daughters are born. To the outside world Omar shows himself to be a very charming person, but indoors he is a tyrant for Jacky. Bit by bit Jacky realizes that she has neither parental nor other rights over her children, neither other rights, and is totally dependent on her husband. Abuse results in a miscarriage. Out of shame, Jacky keeps her situation as a beaten wife a secret from her parents and friends. When she complains to her husband about a rape by a drunken brother-in-law, her husband is furious and beats her. It's her own fault, how dare she talk about his brother in this way! Rapes like this are a terrifying thought for daughters-in-law who reside in an extended family.

Jacky meets other British brides who live in very different circumstances. Some of them married rich men and lead luxurious lives, while others like her are treated badly. Two British women find out they married the same man without knowing it. Bringing charges for bigamy does not stand a change. Thanks to the help of friends, Jacky succeeds in escaping the country to England with her daughters via Israel. She has lived in Egypt for seven years. When Omar finds out, he threatens her. Her problems are not over. She did not get a birth certificate for the younger daughter, so there no official proof that she is the mother. The daughter only can apply for official papers after coming of age.

Source: Jacky Trevane, *Fatwa,* Vianen, The House of Books 2004

Jacky Trevane is not the only one who meets with this fate. In a case like hers, there is no real separation period. When the most important decision of one's life is taken like a step in the dark, the price to pay is no a proper farewell from the past.

Transition

The second phase, transition, is characterized by feelings of uneasiness and homesickness, but also with the start of genuine interest and curiosity about the new environment. After these feelings are dealt with, there is room to value and appreciate the new impressions.

Reintegration

In this period the new bride is more balanced and better able to find her own way.

In the partly biographic novel of Hülya Cigdem, a Turkish bride thinks that marriage with her cousin in the Netherlands will be a one way ticket to a heavenly life. The disenchanting reality is described full of cynical humor. The themes are about the vicissitudes of the lives of young women in Turkey and in the Netherlands, about the daily reality of living with in-laws, lack of personal freedom, lack of stimulus for further development, and other problems an import bride faces. Like lack of privacy, dealing with the spouse who does not fight his mother's demands, he gives in. The mother keeps the salary of her married children. The children must ask her permission for spending their own earnings for their personal use. This situation goes on for years. The grandchildren are the concern of the grandmother as well. She decides what they eat, what they wear, where they attend school, and so on. The husband goes his own way and leaves her alone; the young wife suffers from feelings of loneliness.

According to the author, she encounters more backwardness in the Dutch surroundings than with comparable families in Turkey. Every day is a struggle for survival, without proper plans for the future. The family members constantly remind her that family honor is the highest good in life and that she, the young daughter-in-law, is responsible. Many a young women who has to cope with such circumstances gets serious psychological problems and even attempts suicide. These brides feel misunderstood by Dutch aid programs (or think so beforehand).

Source: Hulya Cigdem, *De importbruid* (*The Import Bride*). Amsterdam: Labor Press 2008

Many of the feelings described here are also recognized by Western brides who marry abroad.

3.3 Adaptation experiences of the expat wife

Experiences with the phases of adjustment of expat wives match those of women who go abroad to get married. The situation of an expat wife has many parallels with that of an emigrant bride. The expat husband comes to the new country to do a job, for which the conditions already are prepared. For him, his position is firmly structured. But his wife is on her own to structure her new life. Moreover, the husband can only give her limited support, as he is very busy getting acquainted with his new, demanding job.

Stages of habituation

In *A Wife's Guide* Robin Pascoe outlines the stages of adjustment for expats when settling in their new posting. Unlike migrant brides, expat wives do not feel the need to detach from their old life. They keep ties with their homeland as their residence in the country of posting will be temporary.

For expats too, there are distinct stages in the culture shock drama. The first phase may be called the honeymoon. Everything is new, funny, and exotic, the people are interesting and the expat family only has good intentions. They have come here to do useful work. After all the hustle and bustle of the preparations, they are ready to start now. It is a euphoric feeling.

But after some time phase two creeps in, a lot of things go wrong. Problems arise with transportation, personnel, language, and everything is terribly difficult. Life seems to slip past with a feeling of not belonging anywhere. There are all sorts of negative feelings about the host country, the people, climate, food, the strange language; nothing seems to be right anymore. For the expat wife, there is no one else to complain to than her spouse, who will not feel happy about this. If feelings of loneliness and homesickness are added on top of all this, there is a real crisis. Some wives do not overcome these problems and leave for home.

For the ones who persist, phase three is a recovery period. The knowledge of the language becomes better and the appreciation about everything the new environment has to offer grows.

After this third phase, there is adjustment. The new habits and surroundings are accepted and the expat will feel at home in his / her environment. Now the added value of life in another culture is appreciated.

The men (who come to do work) usually are encouraged to actively support their wives and a pay them lot of attention, because for them the culture shock not only feels different, but also is often tougher than for men. Why, many a man asks himself. Of course I support my wife, that's why I'm married, but what are they whining about?

Well, what wives whine about is that the husband already is fully absorbed in his new job where everything has been prepared for him beforehand, in the midst of welcoming colleagues. Add to this a demanding introductory course, then the husband's time is fully occupied with his own daily program and coping with his own impressions. After coming home, he needs to share his story as well. He can hardly afford to pay attention to the vague (or specific) feelings of unease his wife is coping with. He does not know how.

The husband does not realize or even know what it means for a wife to figure out what she has to do all by herself. He gets work, colleagues and social contacts on a plate, while the wife must find out where to find everything by herself- shops, schools, a job of her own - and how the children and she find new contacts and make friends.

Public space

Is the new location 'female friendly', i.e. that women in public spaces enjoy the same freedom of movement as in their home country, then just finding the way can be enough to feel at home in the new place of residence. Absence of language problems are a help as well. But if the access of women to public space is very limited and thus fundamentally different from her home country, problems start from day one. All European and other Western women, who end up in Islamic countries, mention this point. For men in Islamic countries it is common to carry out many chores for their wives such as shopping, taking her everywhere she wants to go, chores which a man from a Western culture leaves to his wife.

The expat husband and wife carry with them their own norms and values. If these are so different from the host country, it takes some time before they get a grip on the other social codes. She behaves too freely in public without realizing it; he does not understand why he is now burdened with all kinds of errands which she used to take care of herself.

Adjustment difficulties unacknowledged

A second problem is that problems are not recognized as problems. Expat wives and export brides often experience the most embarrassing situations which are not immediately recognized as adjustment difficulties. Many feel uncomfortable without knowing how to deal with it. This irritates other people, who think the newcomer is bad company and whines all the time. She does not appreciate sound advice, and alienates herself from the ones who try to help her. Fortunately this is also a temporary phase. After some time, the expat wife regains her peace of mind and finds herself a place in her new environment.

In 1988, the Dutch geography student Mirjam van Roode stays in Kenya for a three month internship. She falls in love with the country. In 1990 she returns to Kenya on holiday and meets the Kikuyu Njenga, who is the cook of her safari group. After the holidays, they start a long distance relationship till Njenga moves to the Netherlands, where they marry in 1991. For Mirjam, a university graduate, finding a job in the Netherlands is no problem, but Njenga is 'uneducated' which makes him only eligible for odd jobs. In 1992 Mirjam accepts a job offer in Kenya at an international institute of the United Nations. The young couple returns to Kenya. While she starts her prestigious job, Njenga starts a tourist business. They design and build a house of their own. Mirjam establishes good relations with her Kenyan in-laws and friends. In March 1993, their son Kamau is and born and in September 1994, their daughter Lianne.

Mirjam describes this time as a joyful period. She has interesting work with a large income, and a nice family.

Transition phases with adaptation problems play no role in such circumstances. Mirjam enjoys the status of an expatriate with favorable arrangements. But the relationship with her husband cools down. He does not take it lightly that she earns more than he does, he thinks his friends mock him about this. But is that the real reason? Mirjam does not understand, as he hardly talks about his negative feelings. Does he feel uncomfortable not being able to control her? Is he jealous of her position at a prestigious international organization, which reduces him to the position of 'dependent partner'? Mirjam leaves the marital home in 1997 and moves with the children to a rented house in Nairobi. What follows is a divorce.

When in 1998 her contract ends she returns with her children to the Netherlands. The children have two passports; apparently there are no problems with custody or visitation rights. Mirjam gets a PhD degree at a Dutch university after her research in Kenya.

Ever since, each year Mirjam spends the Christmas holidays with her children in Kenya, to meet Njenga and to visit his family. Back in the Netherlands, feelings of nostalgia never abide.

The Kenyan elections of December 2007 lead to serious riots. In the Western part of the country, the Kikuyu are attacked. The visiting family goes through frightening moments. With difficulty, Mirjam manages to leave safely with her Kikuyu children.

Source: Mirjam van Roode, *The call of the mapori*, Artemis & CO, 2009

3.4 Culture shock at the outset

For women, emigration for marital reasons remains a complex situation. What does the marital state mean, is it a status quo, a goal in life or a final stage of development? For female marriage migrants emigration is a goal in life: they migrate to marry. Once this is accomplished, happiness awaits her, as the thought goes. But what if it feels different and no one in the new environment understands her feelings of insecurity and homesickness?

Loneliness

In the early days of her new life, many a woman feels lonely. However, lonely does not mean alone. Although her husband is busier with his own affairs than with his new wife, the husband's family is so warm that they absorb all her time, her need for some privacy is not understood, and everyone expects her to feel delighted. This attitude may cause feelings of depression, which is not understood either. So, it is very important, in the early stages, to have meaningful activities. But, this is often lacking with feelings of discomfort as a result. It helps to have a job, but this is often made impossible by lack of legal status. Boredom and not being able to communicate properly is a poor start early in a marriage.

Feelings of dependency

Another experience in the early years is dependency, which cannot be evaded. The self-confident and independent woman of yore now is legally and financially dependent on her husband, who in turn depends, or maybe so, of his father. Quite often it turns out that the husband has a lower job position than he has made her believe, which ads to her disappointment. Quite a few women mention this.

Women who had professional careers often feel diminished in these circumstances. Good emotional support from the husband and his environment is essential in this phase.

Preparation

It's not easy to prepare for culture shock. Many brides-to-be hardly give it a thought. If marriage and emigration coincide, the different emotions mingle together and strengthen each other. It is good not to ignore the feelings of culture shock, especially in the initial period but to deal with these. Expressing one's feelings in all stages helps to reflect, to separate from old problems and to focus on the future.

To undertake various activities in a spasmodic way to make you feel useful is not a good strategy. It is better to relax, look around and observe about how life works in the new surroundings. Not only the mind, but also the body must adapt to a different climate with a different lifestyle. Is the new country located in the tropics? Then it can be a shock to learn that the pace of life is so much lower than you are used to and that nobody understands that this is a problem for you. If the weeks before departure were hectic, then being forced to 'doing nothing' feels being hit with a sledgehammer.

3.5 Stabilization

In an unexpected moment, you suddenly feel 'at home'. Sometimes this is so subtle that you don't realize it immediately. The periods of separation, detachment from the old pattern of life, and transition, finding your place in the new environment, are over and you are able now to feel relaxed enough to be pleasant company to others.

Self-confidence

A feeling of growing self-confidence can start during the transition period. The next transition phase, the period of reintegration, in which you start contributing to your new family and environment, seems to follow in a natural way.

Perhaps you will return to your homeland in the future, with or without husband. If so, you then will again go through periods of detachment and re-integration. Of course, at this stage a thought like this is still far away. Anyway, who can predict the course of life?

4 Bones of contention

4.1 Introduction

The meaning of a 'good marriage' is culturally determined. In Western cultures the partners have to build up a good rapport with each other, usually before taking the decision to get wed. That is the basis of a good marriage. But in other, less individualistic cultures, one speaks of a good marriage as when the marriage arrangements are made to the full satisfaction of both parties. There is less need for the partners to know each other well beforehand, this is even considered undesirable. Seen from this point of view, a marriage with an outsider creates a threatening situation. "Marriage to a foreigner always upsets the existing equilibrium in a family. When a marriage takes place between individuals who come from cultures with different marriage practices, such a marriage (...) challenges the very notion of what constitutes a 'proper' marriage."

If so, the foreign bride is met with distrust and reluctance, even more so when the groom ignored his family and took the decision to marry just on his own. His bride will not fit in the clan and meets opposition. Her husband does not want to put his own position in the family clan at further risk and fails to support her.

The Italian woman Sandra Fei meets the Colombian Jaime during his study period at the Italian University of Padua. In 1976 at the age of eighteen she marries him, after which the couple settles in Colombia. The family-in-law does not like her. Soon the relationship with her husband deteriorates. In August 1981, after the birth of two daughters, the younger of the two only six months old, he chases her out of the marital home violently. She has to leave Colombia without her children.

Sandra understands that Jaime's parents consider her a pest to the harmony in the family. "From the very beginning of our marriage, none of the family could afford to accept this stranger, this young outsider. I was not one of them; I stood for independence, I was a threat. I wanted a love relationship with my husband, a relationship on an equal footing, but such a wish fell beyond their comprehension. I was not up to their standards. On every possible occasion they showed their disapproval to Jaime. He had made a mistake by marrying me. A woman who does not respect the clan's rules is a danger. Jaime had damaged the reputation of his family. During Jaime's stay in Italy, far from his family with all their intrigues, he seemed to live a normal life. But he could not resist the pressure of his mother when back in Colombia. After he sent me away in his frenzy, there was no way back for him. Therefore, he claimed that I had left him and the children. With these lies he washed himself clean and was able to return to the family as the prodigal son. Our previous feelings of love were over and could not protect me anymore."

Source: Sandra Fei, *Kidnapped.* Weert: M7P 1993

If the woman gets to know her husband in her own familiar surroundings, she does not realize that living with him in his country will be very different. Dina Khan discusses the identity crisis from Western brides after following their Pakistani husbands to their country. The change in gender roles - the woman undergoes limitations, the man fits again to his old environment - appears to be a turning point in the relationship. "Faced with the choice between conforming or being ostracized by the community, the husband almost always returns to the fold. What was previously considered acceptable behavior for his wife and children now becomes a cause for disagreement. This has happened to many foreign wives."

Difference in status of the young married couple

The stunning ease with which the man fits again "in the bosom of the family ' and fails to support his wife with her adjustment problems often is mentioned.

But, for the man the return to his homeland after a period of study or work abroad is not always easy either. He not only has broadened his views in a way unfamiliar to his family and friends, but on returning he brings in a 'foreign' wife as well. Yet, he comes back in his familiar environment. His foreign period is a thing of the past and he resumes his old routine. His status as 'first class citizen' is not affected in his home country.

For his young wife the situation is different. If she felt herself a "first class citizen' in her home country, then her position on the social status ladder now has dropped three steps: immigrant, woman and daughter-in-law. She is a stranger, of the female sex; and a yet childless daughter-in-law, who in the traditional oriented family-in-law is entitled to the lowest position.

The young and just-married wife usually is totally unaware of this. She assumes she will be judged on her personal qualities and behavior and intends to do her utmost to make a favorable impression.

4.2 External bones of contention

Tensions in a heterogamous marriage can be of an external or an internal nature. External factors relate to differences in national legislation, but might also come from negative comments from the environment of the couple. Rejection of the ethnically mixed partner from the side of parents and friends puts a strain on the marriage relationship. But who gets the blame? By finding out we discover a still unknown gender problem. Firstly, it is women who are on the receiving end of criticisms from the outside world, rather than their men. The second remarkable fact is that it does not matter who of the two of them is the foreign partner. Within both combinations, as a foreign bride in the husband's country or as a woman with a foreign husband in her home country, it is the woman, who has to take the brunt of criticism. On top of this, the criticisms mostly come from the side of other women rather than men.

Accountability

Dutch women married to or cohabiting with a 'foreign' man, are held accountable for their choice of partner by other Dutch people, often women. Not only had the Stichting Lawine ('Avalanche Foundation') found out that Dutch women married to foreigners, are regarded as *wives from foreigners*. Other European countries report similar messages. According to a British source: 'It is against married women rather than men that most criticisms are targeted' (Breger & Hills 1998, p. 96). A German source: "Dabei ist offensichtlich die Konfliktbelastung in Ehen einer deutschen Frau mit einem Ausländer bedeutend grösser als in Ehen zwischen einem deutschen Mann und einer Ausländerin". Moreover, the self-help associations for foreign brides in Germany are organized by German women who themselves are married to foreigners.

Why does this happen to women? Is it a feminine quality to feel more responsible for the justification of the choice of a partner? Or is to confront women more than men a natural thing? The life stories give few answers.

But it must be said that this mental burden for women is in line with the customary law of patriarchal societies. Customary law holds the view that the main responsibility for marital success and happiness lies with the woman. It is her task to serve and please her husband.

4.3 Internal sticking points

Worldwide, there are three classical internal factors for marital problems. These concern money matters, sex and romance, and the upbringing of the children.

Money

In relationships in which partners are on equal footing and have a joint income, usually conflicts are about the expenditure of the family income. What can we afford, can we save on household expenses, how do we spend our vacation? The emphasis is on *us*.

But in relationships where this equivalence is lacking and there is no separate nuclear family income either, the conflicts are of a different nature. Some husbands are generous and give their wives free access to the credit card without prior demands or comments afterwards. But it can also be quite different. In a patriarchal system is no communal family property, each family member looks after his or her own assets. The husband decides about household expenditures. If he is employed in the family business, or lives with his parents, then the head of the family (his father, uncle or brother) makes the final decision on how much money is spent and on what. A foreign spouse without assets has no say at all and feels treated like an infant. This theme recurs in many of the biographies, like in the books about Egypt from Hanneke Rozema and Heike Wagner. Should the husband die, a male guardian takes over the tasks of the deceased, so there is no change in dependency for the remaining widow. Egyptian wives have their own methods to avoid or circumvent unwanted tutelage, for example by secretly holding back money to create small funds for their own use. Men always suspect such actions and feel that wives cannot be trusted.

It is clear that when a "mixed" couple disagrees about spending money, cultural differences - differences in power or opinion about the meaning of a family income –magnify these problems.

Margalith Kleijwegt writes about Sofia. Sofia, born and raised in Rotterdam, Netherlands, with Moroccan parents, lives in a quandary: she is under pressure from her parents (father) to live decently and to marry a groom from Morocco or other Muslim descent, in due time. But these demands clash with her ideas about personal freedom. Her father encourages her to study, which Sofia zealously does, but dad cannot, or does not want to, acknowledge that modern studies require access to a modern lifestyle as well. He rejects the Dutch lifestyle as too free and inappropriate. He does not accept that Sofia has fallen in love with a Dutch boyfriend. As her father behaves more radical, Sofia becomes more rebellious. Her boyfriend Martin does not understand why he is not welcome in Sofia's family.

When Sophia runs away from home her family is in shock. Her mother does not want to break off the contacts with her daughter, but to her father she is equal to a dead person. Sofia and Martin marry in grand style, according to Sofia's wish. But their fresh marriage faces a lot of problems. They fight about money. Both still are students with a limited income to spend. Sofia has a small job as a saleswoman and has received some money from her mother. She spends her money on luxury items like a nice bag, or a lovely weekend outing. Martin strongly disagrees; they can hardly meet their regular household expenses. But Sofia thinks she is free to spend her own money as she wishes. That is according to her Moroccan upbringing. Martin thinks she has a hole in her pocket and runs up unnecessary debts. So, a 'regular' point of dispute gets a cultural load. Is either of them right or wrong, or are both of them right or wrong? Both act according to their own cultural backgrounds. Unfortunately, the problems continue to pile up and the marriage does not last.

Source: Margalith Kleijwegt, *Sofia. Story of a forbidden love.* Amsterdam: Atlas 2010

If the couple has no independent income, but eats at the communal family table and the wife herself lacks income or assets of her own as well, she then entirely depends on what the husband's family is able or willing to spend on her. But things can be arranged different. It is possible to make pre-nuptial agreements in which a future bride lays down her special needs and wishes about financial arrangements. But foreign brides often fail to do so. As a result, the reality is that it is just the husband who decides how much money is spent and on what. He is obliged to do so, as he carries the final responsibility for all things concerning his nuclear family.

Even in marriages where the husband is the marriage migrant in his wife's country, we see this pattern. Often it is customary for the man to send money to his family in his homeland. His wife is not opposed to this financial support, but holds the opinion that caring for their own nuclear family has priority, and that there are not always funds left over to support the family overseas. This practice is a cause for conflicts.

Self-determination

The right to self-determination in a patriarchal family is explained as follows. The father of the household, the patriarch, exercises authority over his wife, his children, and partners of his children, and grandchildren, who all belong to his household. He has the final say on all decisions, which are not discussed. This does not mean he is just playing boss, but because he carries the final responsibility for the welfare and state of affairs in his family. The same principle applies in other areas, such as the workplace. Contradicting the boss is not done. If all goes well, the praise is for the father or the boss, while in case of wrongdoings from the side of his family members or staff, it is he who gets the blame and has to solve the conflict. The hierarchy in the family structure is a clear one: women are under the authority of men, younger generations under the authority of older generations. The status of a woman in the family circle depends on the phase of life. As a child, she falls under the authority of her parents and grandparents, as a young married woman not only under the authority of her husband and his father, but also of her mother-in-law. Once she is a mother herself, she raises one step higher, and after her children are married she becomes a mother-in-law in her own right, and has to carry all responsibility for the ins and outs of the large household.

Like men, women are expected to spend most of their time with members of the same sex. For the foreign spouse, two more changes concerning her situation of self-determination are added. The women, whose company she shares, are not her own choice. They are members of his family, and sisters-in-law married into the family, so no relatives or friends of hers. On top of this comes the restriction of the freedom of movement for women, who mainly spend their days indoors. The reason behind this restriction is the need to protect women against the 'dangers of the outside world'.

A good father, who stands confident and relaxed in life, deals with this requirement lightly, and allows his wife and daughters plenty of personal space with as few limitations as possible.

But the opposite also occurs: many a man fulfills his duties by keeping the females of his family very restricted and monitors everything they do. Such a man treats his wife and children as his personal possessions, like livestock. All family members have to serve him and conform to his rules without any comment. Men like that do not tolerate a wife's wish for a divorce. If so, their pride is hurt severely. They might stalk the ex-wife and kidnap the children.

This asymmetry in the marriage relationship is highly consequential and often leads to fights. The man demands accountability from his wife, but refuses to be so to her in return. The woman complains that her husband commands her, just goes his own way and hardly involves her in his life. She also finds out that he takes important decisions, such a moving house, buying property or matters concerning the education of their children, on his own and informs her later on. He says he does not want to overburden her with trivialities, but who decides what a trifle is and what is not?

Women in a quandary

The lack of self-determination is also, often painful, perceptible in the public space. The streets are populated by men. 'Stray' women are harassed, accosted and shouted at. It makes women feel uncomfortable, out of place.

So, not only self-determination, but also freedom of movement gets a very different meaning for the Western woman.

Women's rights have two angles which are perpendicular to each other. So the position of women is in a quandary. Her rights in the secular field - vote, own job, participation in legal matters - clash with the constraints of the religion-based family law, where the husband or father has the final say over the freedom of movement of a wife or daughter. Sooner or later, each Western wife gets stuck in this dichotomy. But it is not only she who is affected. Her husband feels the dilemma as well, as he is forced to make contradictory decisions. Should he allow his wife the freedom of movement she is used to in her own culture, or forbid her this because of the negative reactions he expects? What to do to guard the family honor without losing his authority as head of the family?

A German woman, who after a four-year marriage to an Egyptian man wants a divorce, puts such a situation as follows: "Throughout the marriage, both of us became mentally worn out. A European woman as a girlfriend was nice, but a marriage required too much effort. His independence and privileges as an Egyptian male were at stake. He had to defend and explain his behavior to me all the time, and I failed to obey him silently.

Conversely, the same was true for me. My husband was a very charming and sociable person, but to stay at home all day waiting for him and be ready for him, was inconsistent with my ideas on gender equality. Both of us had to give in too much and there were too many new obligations, which impaired us to be happy. In every marriage you have to make concessions, but the roles of men and women in Egypt differed too much from what I was used to. I cannot adapt to a life with so many different obligations without pain."

Source: Hanneke Rozema, *Boundless love*. Amsterdam: Bulaaq 2005

For people from a patriarchal culture, these customs and traditions are so common, even for those who hold different opinions, that they do not realize how problematic the limitations in lifestyle can be for the foreign woman. But even if the husband informs his wife in advance, neither can imagine how this translates in their everyday life. The wife thinks the restrictions will not apply to her; she will do as she pleases and don't let herself be patronized by pesky etiquette rules or habits in the family. Moreover, her husband also assured her that he will not restrict her. But, being once again incorporated into the family, life changes. The husband, who during his stay abroad acted so independently, cannot escape the ruling hierarchy. He has to respect the orders and wishes of his father and cannot question the authority of his mother over the daughter-in-law. "Sorry, honey, I also wished things were different. But I am on my way now, see you tonight. " No further discussion...

Sex and romance

Few authors write about the sexual aspects of their marriage, but there are facts found between the lines. So, to show outward signs of affection, like holding hands, kissing in public or in front of family members, all of this is 'not done'. To express romantic feelings outside the bedroom is ridiculous behavior for a man. As loss of face is a fatal blow for a man, everyone takes care this never happens.

Many a biography writer says that in bed, her husband acts as the one who is entitled to sex. He demands and she gives in, a wife can never refuse a husband's sexual demands.

Ideas about sexuality are dominated by a double standard. Young men are encouraged to get sexual experience, but at the same time, require their future spouse to be a virgin. Although it is common knowledge that this is not always realistic, the virginity myth is still alive.

There is information from an unsuspected source about what foreign wives can expect. In her book *The men of the Netherlands,* the Frenchwoman Sophie Perrier interviewed several foreign (ex-) wives of Dutch men about their married life in the Netherlands.

The foreign partners describe the Dutch man as physically attractive and athletic, friendly and very reliable. He is not macho, that's pretty much an insult to him. He is no womanizer, he cannot flirt very well. He is not romantic, compliments are seldom heard. High-spirited arguments are wasted on him as annoying behavior.

For him, gender equality is fundamental in the relationship. He won't live a double life, which he thinks too complicated. He treats his wife as his equal and fully involves her in all marital decisions. One woman even sighs: "The men here do not see us as women, but as people." Personal freedom, inside and outside the marriage, are paramount values for him.

As a lover the man is caring and understanding, there is no question of possessive or compulsive behavior. He shows consideration for her wishes. If she has no interest in sex for whatever reason, he accepts that and does not insist. He seems ignorant about jealousy, as he does not object to her talking to 'strange' men. But she does not appreciate this lack of jealousy. The foreign wife thinks he is indifferent, which makes her feel insecure. In more macho oriented societies, jealousy is a sign of love and protection. In short, the caring and reliability of the Dutch man is praised, but at the same time the relationship lacks ups and downs, which hardly makes it sparkling.

The sometimes hilarious description of the peculiarities of the Dutch man as husband and as lover provides a mirror image for the expected marital reality the Dutch woman has. For her a reliable husband is sober and decent, and hardly romantic. He will avoid unpleasant surprises, as he allows her a full say in all family matters. Husband and wife work together on household tasks. She might be as able to fix a tire as he is in changing a diaper.

A Dutch woman takes her own pattern of norms and values of equality and personal fulfillment with her in her marriage. A man in a macho culture does the same with his pattern of values.

Behavior of the husband

Many women report an often unexpected and consequently startling experience about the behavior of their new husband. Once married, nothing is left of his romantic courtship. It's like if he has pulled out a jacket. He is possessive, commands her and puts her firmly under his authority. Sometimes such behavior starts right in or after the wedding night.

The Australian woman Jacqueline Gillespie and the French woman Evelyn Durieux share an experience like this. Both marry a "prince", who possesses few personal qualities and behaves like a despot.

Jacqueline Gillespie meets the Malaysian prince Bahrin, grandson of the Sultan of Terengganu, in Melbourne where he is studying architecture. She is 17, he is 26 years old. Bahrin overwhelms her with luxurious vacations, and other expensive presents before taking her to Malaysia. There they talk about getting married. She is told to answer affirmatively on some question and to sign something. Then it turns out she is married under Islamic law! She claims not to have understood that this was a marriage ceremony, but the commitment is sealed. In the wedding night she feels raped and abused. Her groom demands complete obedience and submission.

In the periods when the couple resides in Australia, Bahrin shows himself a caring and attentive husband. After five years and two children, the marriage is definitely on the rocks. The divorce is arranged in Australia, the children stay with Jacqueline and Bahrin gets visiting rights. But some time later Bahrin kidnaps the children and takes them to Malaysia. Malaysia does not cooperate in bringing them back to their Australian non-Muslim mother.

The French woman Evelyn Durieux grows up in Africa and in France. Her father works in the Central African Republic of President Bokassa. Bokassa's son Georges courts Evelyn. Her parents are against the relationship, but ultimately Bokassa's power of persuasion is too strong. Evelyn is intimidated by the smart Georges. She is nineteen and pregnant when she marries him on 22 February 1975. On the - luxury - wedding day she sees that the marriage document leaves space to list more wives.... From the wedding day onwards Georges exhibits possessive, autocratic behavior. He beats her and behaves just as fickle as his father, for whom he has previously warned her. After ten turbulent years the couple divorces.

Sources: Jacqueline *Gillespie, Yasmin, a fairy tale that became a nightmare.* New York: Tirion 1998

Evelyn Durieux, *The barefoot Princess, love and hate at the court of Emperor Bokassa.* New York: The Core 1993

Almost all export brides mention an, often significant, change in the relation with their husband after the wedding. During the courtship period, he showed himself a witty and thoughtful suitor, who did his utmost to make her happy. After the wedding day that blissful period seems light years away. Now he keeps his distance, literally as well as figuratively. Homey, intimate moments together, become rare. For relaxation and amusement, he seeks the company of other men, brothers and friends. That is the daily routine; it is unusual for husband and wife to sit together for a cozy unpretentious tête-à-tête. Males often meet outdoors, on the market, in the coffee shop or anywhere else. Take a friend home and introduce him to his wife? That is not done.

The man's behavior is shaped by his culture. He treats a woman whom he is courting, whom he is married to, and whom has become a mother, in accordance to the stage in her life. A Western woman, who holds the opinion that her personality does not change while passing through life's changes, hardly appreciates this point of view. So, this experience often is an important topic in the life stories.

Education

The respondents of Perrier say that a Dutch man is a caring, loving and patient father. He spends time with his children and encourages them to think for themselves and ask questions about anything they want to know. But rebuke at misconduct is a task for the (foreign) mother. This observation certainly holds some truth. In international research, Dutch children are classified as noisy and undisciplined, but also as very free and happy.

In a patriarchal society the definition of the different responsibilities of father and mother is clearer. Mother cares and father decides. Children must obey to parental authority. To ask too many questions is not encouraged, but interpreted as challenging the authority of the father, which is rude. When the family lives in an extended family household, the (paternal) grandmother has more say about the education of the children than their own mother. That's a shock to the foreign mother. Added to that, she is expected to educate her children according to the religion, norms and values of her husband's family. This can interfere with her own beliefs.

Children often play a tragic role in the life stories. After a divorce, the father and his family block the contact with the foreign mother. The difficulties of mothers in getting back their children, who were abducted by the father, are the main theme of many a story. Betty Mahmoody, Donya al-Nahi, Loudy Nijhof, Pamela Green, Sandra Fei, Janneke Schoonhoven, these and other mothers have found out that the poetic expression: "she gives, donates, children to her husband" has a very literal meaning.

In the late eighties, the American woman Betty Mahmoody's *Not without my daughter* is published. She describes her marriage to Moody, an Iranian doctor who has settled in the United States of America. They get married in 1977. In September 1979, their daughter is born. In August 1984, Betty accompanies her husband with their young daughter on a family visit to Iran. But, in Iran, Moody confronts her with his decision to remain there. Harassment and intimidation follow, Betty feels caged. Her American nationality has no legal meaning in Iran; her status is that of the wife of an Iranian man. Does the husband refuse to let her travel to America? Then she gets no passport and no ticket.

In the meantime in Iran, the mood is very anti-American. The infamous fourteen-month siege of the U.S. embassy staff in Tehran, which ended in January 1981, is still fresh in the Iranian mind. Ever since, the American embassy is closed, and Switzerland represents the interests of the United States.

After some time, Betty's husband agrees to let her go, but not with their daughter. He guards both of them closely. In the meantime, Betty learns the local Farsi language and studies the Koran. In secret she devises a plan to escape together with her little daughter. With the help of Iranian and Kurdish friends Betty succeeds in fleeing to Turkey in February 1986. The winter trip from Tehran to Ankara, with taxis, on horseback and on foot with Kurdish guides, is written as a blood-curdling adventure.

Back in America, Betty writes her famous book, which later was made into a feature film. Book and movie hit like a bombshell in circles of ethnically mixed marriages. Other women acknowledged Betty's story. Married in America to foreign men, they also found out later that they hardly knew anything about the culture of their husbands. But Betty gets venomous criticisms as well. She is accused of putting Iran and the Iranian men in a bad light. The critics see her as a woman, who is frustrated about her failed marriage.

But this was not Betty's intention at all. She has a positive opinion about the happy years she enjoyed with her husband as well as about the help she gets from warm-hearted Iranians. She wants to point out how a mixed marriage can have an unexpected outcome. American women like her who marry foreigners, meet them in the United States. Usually, the man studies or works, he is familiar with the English language and gives the impression he wants to stay in the country. If so, the American wife does not feel the need to get familiar with his background. But there comes a time he returns to his homeland and abuses the fundamental rights the wife enjoys in her home country. Be prepared, that is the message from Betty Mahmoody.

Source: Betty Mahmoody, *In een sluier gevangen Not without my daughter.* Weert: M&P 1987

4.4 The Future

No society is static, and patriarchal societies have their own dynamics as well. Modern information technology has reached the most obsolete corners of the world. Virtual doors are open for girls and women to get an education or a job without impeding the strict purdah-rules which keep women at home. In Morocco, discussion is going on about family law, women claim more rights, such as the right for divorce. In the highly conservative country Saudi-Arabia there are developments as well. Saudi girls go to school and hold jobs later on. Besides accessible jobs in education and health care, there are new opportunities in commerce and banking. These women do not feel suppressed at all. They have their own ways to get what they want.

Rajaa Alsanea writes about the lives of four friends from the Saudi capital Riyadh. The girls hail from the top of society. The book is about their daily routine of joys and sorrows. Their lives are fully programmed with university studies and travels to Europe and America. The old-fashioned traditions in the strictly separated worlds of men and women in Saudi are put down in a hilarious way. It is about romances, secret relationships, sexual desires, family and relations, all that concerns young women. The items about flirtations, and falling in love, are paramount. Young unmarried people do succeed in meeting each other, girls with a foreign driving license disguised as men take the wheel, the secret exchange of telephone numbers, and all these adventures are highly interesting. Although women have little freedom of movement in public life, this seems not to bother the book's main characters. But they can make use of chauffeur-driven cars, which is a great help.

A young man in love abandons his beloved when his mother disapproves of the match. The man is highly educated and self-supporting, but it is impossible for him not to comply with his mother's wish. The girlfriends frown upon his behavior. Another young man, who studies in America and has met an American girlfriend, marries the bride his family has arranged for him when he is home in Riyadh for a family visit. Back in the United States with his new wife, the wife scorns the American girlfriend. Then the man sends his wife back to Saudi and divorces her. As a divorced status damages a woman's reputation, the girlfriends discuss how wrongly treated this bride was.

The stories put another light on the ingrained prejudices of the suffocating restrictions for women in Saudi. They have their own ways to cope with independence and search for happiness.

Source: Rajaa Abdulla Alsanea, *The girls of Riyadh*. Amsterdam: Archipel 2008

But, progressive or not, in the minds of people ideas and habits of traditional times, persist for a long time. It is no surprise to see that people stick to rules and customs from the past. This happens everywhere, even in the most modern of societies.

PART III

AVOIDING PROBLEMS

5 Family law

5.1 Introduction

To answer the question about how the ideas and realities about marriage change, we should put in a nutshell how Dutch marriage laws of the past two centuries have developed. We compare the legalities of the Dutch marriage laws with Islamic and other patriarchal legal systems. Since the foundation of the Kingdom of the Netherlands in 1813 in the Dutch marriage laws have seen a lot of changes.

We go back to the international feminist movements of the late nineteenth century, in which Dutch women also played a role. The more recent developments of the late twentieth and early twenty-first century in patriarchal cultures have quite a few parallels with the situation of our Western society in the aforementioned period.

5.2 Development of Dutch marriage laws

The French occupation of 1795-1813, saw a fundamental change in the Dutch civil legal system. It laid the basis for the modern marriage legislation, starting with the separation of Church and State in 1796. From that year onwards, marriages had to be civilly registered.

Marital Status

In the nineteenth century, the social position of women was closely linked to their marital status. Two types of individuals were distinguished: those with full legal capacity and those without. The second category, called *personae miserabiles*, consisted of minors of both sexes, persons under guardianship and married women. The *personae miserabiles* enjoyed the special protection of the state because they could not represent themselves in legal matters. Moreover, they were at the same time protected 'against themselves' by the father, guardian, or husband, who represented them.

The married woman as a *persona miserabilis* had a special place. Although it was not denied that she, technically speaking, was able to act legally, her subject status came out of her free will. The woman relinquished those rights voluntarily, although without a chance to negotiate it. As already mentioned, the father not only had the authority, but also the whole responsibility for the welfare of women and children. In the patriarchal world of the nineteenth-century divorce was inappropriate. A good patriarch took care to prevent such a catastrophe.

The legislation did recognize the need to protect women against the adverse consequences of their inferior position, but changing that position was impossible. Unmarried adult women were legally competent. Divorced and widowed women regained the rights they 'voluntary' ceded. Although the marital state had disadvantages for a woman, to remain unmarried was even less enviable. A woman only became fully human if she married. But as that was detrimental to her civil liberty she got into a paradoxical situation. To say it cynically: "Only after the death of the husband, the woman is a real human being, she has freedom of movement, she can manage her own finances, and she gets custody rights over her children."

Patriarchal marital power

A family structure like this only flourishes in an authoritarian and traditional patriarchal system. The patriarchal style is partly legitimized by the generally older age of the male spouse. Also most other cultures make a conscious choice for a younger wife for the same reason, to allow the man a better chance to exercise authority.

In everyday life, the married man represents his family in legal matters without consulting his wife as she is legally incompetent. The man manages the family finances, determines where his family resides, and has the final decision on the upbringing and education of the children. The man should lead his wife, the wife obeys her husband. If a man marries a foreign woman she takes the nationality of her husband and loses her own. A woman who marries a foreign man must renounce her own nationality and gets the one of the spouse. This is desirable for the unity of the family.

Women and girls appear in public as little as possible. That's inappropriate. The working class women do so, but they have a lower position in society. In paintings and photographs of urban life from the nineteenth century one hardly sees 'ladies' in the streets, but male laborers and 'gentlemen' and women who work as maids and nannies.

For men, entering into a marriage marks the social transition to adulthood and empowerment.

An Arabian Princess Between Two Worlds would never have been written if the author, Princess Salme bint Said from Zanzibar (1844 -1924) had obeyed the strict conventions of her country and time. However, she takes the highly unusual step to marry a foreign, non-Muslim man. Around 1866 she meets Heinrich Ruete, a merchant from Hamburg, Germany. Much to the dislike of Salme's family, a romance blossoms. A relationship with a non-Muslim foreign man is not only impossible, but even a mortal sin. Salme get the advice 'to go on a pilgrimage', a journey from which she will not return, or is this only a whisper? It's a fact that Salme secretly sells her assets, and despite an imposed house arrest leaves Zanzibar on a dark night on a British ship. She goes to Aden, where she remains for almost a year. Ruete settles his affairs in Zanzibar before he rejoins her a few months later. In the meantime Salme has a child, and receives instruction about the Christian faith. May 30, 1867 is a memorable day: she is baptized and takes the name Emily, marries Ruete, and sets sail with him for Europe.

Later, when her three children in Germany grow up without contact with their mothers' family, they hear from strangers that their mother is an Arab princess. Salme then takes up the pen to write about the memories of her childhood in Zanzibar. Her book is published as: *Memoiren einer Arabischen Prinzessin.* "Letters Home", the letters she writes about her life in Germany to an (unknown), girlfriend or sister in Zanzibar, are added later.

Salme's stories about the differences in lifestyles in nineteenth century Zanzibar and Germany are very interesting. The description of her feelings of fear and confusion about life between two cultures is touching.

Her experiences are still very recognizable in our time. Salme compares habits and customs of both cultures in which she shows herself a sharp observer. She not only speaks of Western or Eastern, or European or African, but uses the currently most modern designation 'the South' for her homeland, and "the North" for Germany and Europe in general.

After arriving in Germany the fear of the unknown overwhelms her, everything is strange and she understands nothing. She wants to learn German as quickly as possible in order not to look stupid or uneducated. The people might think that all Arabs are that way. With the knowledge of the German language and customs she discovers new and charming customs: at Christmas time not only the children get presents, but children also give presents to their father and mother. Her father Said never was that happy, he only shared his gifts without getting anything in return. Moreover, the giver decides himself about his gifts, instead of delegating this task to servants.

Salme shows great appreciation for the German system of financial management. Even young children learn how to deal with money. They start with pocket money and are held accountable about the spending of it.

About education, she thinks there is too much emphasis on sharpening the mind, while the development of feelings, of character, is neglected. As soon as children go to school, they are lost to their parents. Many of the hours spent in school, could be used in a better way at home to develop their characters. But it cannot be helped; school attendance is a legal obligation. With these comments, Salme indicates how difficult it is for a foreign parent to bring up her children according to the laws and norms of another country and culture.

Salme's personal experiences with empowerment and self determination are at odds with the perception that women of her culture are held incapable. Still in Zanzibar, she was declared of age as a twelve year old and was solely responsible for the management of her own inherited estates and property. But when she becomes a widow later in Germany, she is not entitled to direct control of the inheritance of her husband. That task is to be left to male guardians.

It is a striking fact that Salme, in line with spirit of her time, leaves the double standard on gender inequality outside discussion. Her father Said had dozens of concubines and children. His first (and only lawful) wife was of equal rank, she always kept the first place in the polygamous marriage. Said bought slaves as concubines, Salme's mother being one of them. But all his children were princes and princesses with equal legal status. Her father accepted full responsibility for the welfare and prosperity of all his wives and children. The non-Muslim wives were not forced to convert, although that certainly was appreciated. But an Islamist, who converted to another faith, committed a mortal sin. A pregnancy outside wedlock, which happened to Salme, was a mortal sin as well. Her male relatives, however, could do so without sanctions. But not she. Salme could not stay in Zanzibar; she had to leave her country like a thief in the night.

Source: Sayyida Salme / Emily Ruete, *An Arabian Princess Between Two Worlds*. Brill Publishers, Leiden 1992

Father's will is the law

In the Netherlands, the nineteenth century is the heyday of the patriarchal system. The influence of the state stops there, where the influence of the father begins. A historical incident from 1872 illustrates the paternal authority. On February 9, 1870 the then 17 year old Aletta Jacobs writes a letter to the Minister of Home Affairs, Mr. Thorbecke, and requesting admission to the University of Groningen. She wants to become a physician and believes that there is nothing in *the Act on higher education* that excludes women. Thorbecke asks her if she realizes what the study involves and whether her father knows of her plans. Aletta informs her father and the minister also asks him his opinion on the matter. When Aletta's father answers that he stands by his daughter, the minister supports her request. Thorbecke says in parliament: 'If the father has no objection, what right has the Minister to refuse?" So, Thorbecke endorses the paternal power. The story goes that Minister Thorbecke personally authorized Aletta's admission to the university, which was his last ministerial decision before he died. Strictly speaking this was not so, as there was no need for additional legislation. The Minister only endorsed the views of Aletta's father.

However, the minister's statement is seen as a turning point in the history of women's rights. After Aletta Jacobs, the first Dutch woman to enter university, higher education stands open to women.

5.3 Feminism

The end of the nineteenth century sees a rapidly changing society. Women become better educated and articulate enough to stand up for their legal and social position. It happens that men from 'higher circles', who are well educated and hold responsible positions in society, marry late or not at all. One explanation is that they think marriage is too expensive: the potential partners from the same higher classes are brought up in luxury and idleness, and expect to continue such a lifestyle when married. This in contrast to the women of the 'working class' and peasants: these wives contribute to the household income which make them desirable spouses. But the higher class girls are caught in a stalemate. Their upbringing as economic "non-valeurs" makes then unattractive brides, while at the same time marriage is their only destiny.

There is opposition to this compulsory idleness. The upcoming women's movement grabs the dilemmas of the legal and social inequality. The so-called first wave of feminism is a fact. Cécile Goekoop-de Jong van Beek en Donk (1866-1944) is one of the leading ladies. Like Aletta Jacobs (1854-1929), she is an active member in the Association for Women's Suffrage. The ladies also promote better training for girls to make them able to earn their own living.

In her novel about *Hilda van Suylenburg,* published in 1897, author Cécile Goekoop elaborates on issues which still, more than a century later, are surprisingly modern and up to date. We recognize "the smart girl, who is prepares on her future', *avant la lettre*. The emerging ideas about empowerment and equal gender rights meet with strong opposition as undesirable modernism. It is just blah-blah, eccentric behavior, and turns the world upside down.

"What is emancipation, which now so often is talked about, Mom?" - "What that is, my child? Yes, that's such an idea to make a woman more like a man, who goes to the polls with a cigar in her mouth, while the man stays at home to look after the children." The social position of men and women is as it is. And why should girls make themselves useful and develop their talents? Marriage is her destiny. A woman who works to earn money behaves in an unfeminine way and shames her husband or father. If women have nothing to do because they are not allowed to, why not make visits to poor families as a pastime?

However, it is a fact that many a woman has to work to maintain herself and her needy family. But the better-paid jobs are not open to her. For female breadwinners there is only poorly paid work, which is often also dangerous for her health, about this, no one protest about unfeminine behavior.

'Silent poverty "is the fate of women with small incomes. From the perspective of social justice it would therefore be preferable to deny wealthy young men access to the better paid jobs. Those men do not need that money. And if this is impossible, why not establish funds for female breadwinners, so that these women do not have to go to work?

Bad moral behavior of men is condoned, but women are resented if they act the same way. There is a double standard of morality and decency. The destiny for women is marriage. But if a young woman is active and calculating looking for a suitable partner, a wealthy man with good prospects, she behaves contemptibly in the eyes of her own sex. A girl should enter marriage with high ideals of love and conviction. And men believe that girls should wait passively for a proposal, while they consider girls who do so, as dull. Mothers, who educate their daughters to be passive, complain that the daughters have no skills at all.

A female doctor is outraged about the fact that a poor unmarried seventeen-old girl falls pregnant, while the father, a man in a high position, leaves her to her fate. There is no legal way to force the man to care for mother and child. "Those kind of men should look at Mohammedans, who are openly polygamous, but care for all their wives and children."

The fact that the legal position of married women is equal to that of criminals, lunatics and children is ridiculous. How far does the requirement of complete obedience of a wife to her husband go? Suppose a wife obeys her husband who wants her to commit a murder. A judge would acquit her? This legal position is outrageous!

The law must be changed to remove injustice. But that's not enough. Women need to work hard to improve their position and not just complain and blame others. Women are able enough to claim their rights. Female associations will help in the struggle for better conditions and to compete with men. Women will be happier and work without bitterness. The main character of Hilda van Suylenburg commits herself to the feminist movement. Against all prejudices, she completes law school, after which she assists poor women as a pro bono lawyer.

Source: Cécile Goekoop-de Jong van Beek en Donk, *Hilda van Suylenburg,* 1897

The overview of the history of marriage law and gender emancipation in the nineteenth century shows that Western countries, like the Netherlands, also once knew a patriarchal family system. Today, such a system is no longer legally supported and largely forgotten. But knowledge about the past gives a better understanding of present day patriarchal system in other parts of the world. Elements of Western patriarchal societies from our past are still very much alive today in other countries.

5.4 Preparation for marriage

It is a universal truth that marriage as an institution stands in high regard. A bachelor is but half a man. However, the character of relationships changes. The Dutch Family Council points out: "Unmarried cohabitation, usually as precursor to marriage, has increased sharply. Young people at first live alone or in cohabitation, although this is only temporary. Marrying straight from the parental home is out'. The postponement of marriage and parenthood, and pursuing diverse lifestyles is the trend. Since the divorce procedure is simplified, divorce became an ordinary termination of contract. However, the findings of the Dutch Family Council may not be true for Dutch immigrants. In immigrant circles early marriages are still common.

5.5 Information or warning

"It is recommended that the registrar of the marriage record does not just indicate the price differences between a wedding with or without a red carpet, but gives information on the legal and economic aspects of the marriage."

Source: De Hoog, *Selection of marriage partners in the Netherlands,* 1982.

Information

Adequate information for making an informed decision hardly exists. Information is seen as a warning. According to Dienke Hondius (1999), her respondents only felt irritated by warnings. "Cynically put, a bride forewarned is not a bride forearmed, like the famous saying goes, but is left to her own devices. A warning to mixed couples appears to be the announcement of a distance. Family and friends turn away from the couple. But the warnings were quite reasonable, as mixed marriages more often lead to divorce."

We must conclude that a systematic information channel that is well known and accessible enough to clarify the consequences of getting married does not exist, and even less so for international or inter-ethnic couples.

Dutch and other Western girls, who intend to get married to men from exotic countries, often receive a lot of well-intentioned advice from all sides. But that gives them little hold. The effect is rather that a bride does not feel supported, but attacked, which makes her more determined than ever to proceed with the marriage arrangement of her own choice. Each comment is considered a criticism. In a later chapter, we see the pitfalls of such an attitude.

5.6 Separation of Church and State

In most Western countries Church and State are separated. A difference in religion between marriage partners is no impediment to marriage. In daily life, all citizens are free in their religious beliefs, as a religious belief is considered a personal choice. In family law, religion plays no role. A church wedding is possible as a personal choice, but a religious ceremony is not compulsory.

Officials in matrimonial law

The *registrar*, a government official, has the sole authority to conclude a civil marriage. But at the dissolution of the marriage through death of one partner, another official is required. A *notary* settles the estate for the surviving partner and other heirs. If the marriage is dissolved by divorce, then a *judge* decides about the arrangements, such as alimony and custody of children under age. In case of disagreement, a *magistrate of a juvenile court* intervenes. So, a multitude of officials are involved in the various stages of a marriage.

5.7 Family law and religion

How different is family law in a country like Morocco.

Each religion follows its own legal system. For Muslims the family law, the Mudawwana, is based on the Qur'an. A marriage is solemnized in the presence of two udul, Moroccan notaries. After negotiations with both parties, they write down the contribution of the spouses-to-be. An adult man negotiates for himself, while the bride or minor groom is represented by a marriage guardian. However, the bride must agree and sign by herself. There is no distinction between a civil and a religious marriage. The woman is entitled to a bride price, to be paid by the groom. A non-Muslim spouse is an impediment to a marriage for Muslim women, but not for a Muslim man.

Community of goods does not exist in this system. Within marriage, the partners don't have an equal position; the wife is subject to the authority of her husband. The man is obliged to support his wife, while she is entitled his support and protection. A man can divorce his wife if he wants to, but a woman is very restricted should she want to step out of her marriage. A divorce is arranged and negotiated by the udul, according to the agreements from the marriage contract. The obligation to maintain a wife ends at the end of the marriage. A right to alimony or inheritance is not obvious, even less so for a non-Muslim wife.

Asymmetric marriage

The Islamic marriage relationship is asymmetric: the man represents his wife in the outside world, takes part on her behalf in legal transactions, and has the final say in all family matters, while the woman owes her husband obedience. Wife and children are entitled to his care and protection. She has a right to manage her own assets according to her own wish.

The man exercises parental authority over children, the woman has only the right to care for them till a certain age. In case of a divorce, the children remain under the authority of the man, the mother does not gets custody, but her right to care for them is still valid. The same applies if the husband dies, then the mother's only right is to care, without official custody of her minor children.

But it is clear that these rules have long been overtaken by the realities of everyday life. Although marriage as an institution is still held in high regard, marriages are not stable, and divorces are common. It also often happens more and more that a mother is alone, or with the help of her own relatives, in providing for her children. Neither is it an exception if women contribute to the household income through wage labor. But this is a difficult topic to discuss.

Family law and other religions

The description of the Islamic family law in Morocco is broadly consistent with the family law system in other countries of North Africa and Asia. The religious minorities in these Islamic countries, like Christians, Jews, Druze or Hindus, have their own rules in family law for marriage, birth and death. These rules are as patriarchal as those of their Muslim compatriots.

Many rules in these patriarchal family systems, which are based on religion, are diametrically opposed to the legal systems in most Western countries. There, civil law is secular and patriarchal elements have been removed in favor of gender equality.

5.8 Dual nationality and family law

There are two types of legal systems for the granting of a nationality.

In countries with *jus soli* the criterion is the native soil. This means that anyone born in such a country may be entitled to citizenship of that country, irrespective of whether the parents have that same nationality. In most cases, the nationality, obtained by *jus soli*, cannot be waived. The native soil never changes.

In other countries *jus sanguinis* is the rule, which means that a child is entitled to the nationality of its parents, according to the bloodline, even if the child is born outside its parent's home country.

In mixed marriages often a combination of birth rights lead to a double nationality, both for the spouses and the children. Moreover, spouses can often opt for the nationality of the partner. Each country, Western or non-Western, has its own peculiarities with nationality laws.

The occurrence of dual nationality is probably as old as the existence of passports. In many countries a dual nationality is undesirable, but tolerated.

Advantages and disadvantages

Dual citizenship has advantages and disadvantages.

For a woman, who follows her husband to his home country, it may be an advantage to adopt his nationality, as her residence permit and work permit are more secure. If she keeps her own nationality too, she can continue her family visits without visa hassles. The children benefit in the same way from having two passports.

But a dual nationality may also have adverse effects, when the family law of the two nationalities is very different. This point has already been discussed. If there is a dual nationality in a family, the consequences for the men and the women of that family are not the same. Migrants often retain two nationalities. Men can take advantage of the dual legal system at the expense of their wives and daughters. Men are able to abuse their womenfolk with the law at their side. On holiday or on family visit in the Islamic country, a man can decide to leave his wife or daughter there. He takes her passport, she cannot appeal. Conversely, this is not possible: a wife or daughter cannot take her husband's or father's passport, or apply for a new one for herself without his consent. This is an example of gender inequality, sanctioned by (family) law.

The Moroccan girl Karima Ouchan is a victim of patriarchal power. When she is a child her family moves from Morocco to the Netherlands. She is a good student, and as a teenager she wants to escape from her father's grip on her life. She tries to run away from home several times. In 1985, when the family travels to Morocco on holiday, she jumps overboard into the Mediterranean Sea. She is still in High School and will be married off in Morocco. She does not want that. But Karima is rescued from the sea! After her desperate act, her father seems to change his mind and promises her more freedom. Back in the Netherlands Karima resumes her studies. In the same year, the family again travels to Morocco. Then her father shuts her up. Karima stays in Morocco. She withstands all marriage proposals and defies the bad treatment by her family. Secretly, with the help of her brothers who stand by her, she keeps in touch with friends in the Netherlands.

But after years of misery - twelve years! - she returns! Her father allows her to apply for a passport, thinking no one in the Netherlands will welcome her after all these years. But the Dutch authorities grant her a residence permit for humanitarian reasons. On March 29, 1997 she is back. She is 27 years old by now and can continue her education.

The book provides more than one poignant description of how a paterfamilias can abuse his power. Karima's father had chosen his own bride in Morocco against his mother's wish. Later on in the Netherlands, he beats his wife up and sends her back to her parents in her homeland, as she 'has become insane ', then remarries, and takes this wife (stepmother to Karima) to the Netherlands. But he is also a bully to this wife and her children. It is even more distressing that Karima after returning to the Netherlands feels obliged to financially support her father, now he has to care for so many children ...

Source: Karima Ouchan, *The never written letter to my father.* Amsterdam: Bulaaq 1999

Another example of how far the abuse of women to the benefit of male family members goes is the case of the British sisters Zana and Nadia Muhsen. Their British nationality did not protect the girls from the forced marriage their Yemeni father arranged for them. No authority, neither British nor Yemini, held the father accountable. Ever since 1990 their story has been highly publicized with at least three books and much international TV coverage. However, there is no justice for the girls.

The Muhsen sisters grow up in Birmingham with five more siblings. Their Yemeni father and British mother are not married, as their father's marriage in his home country never is dissolved. In 1980 Zana and Nadia are aged fourteen and sixteen years. In that year, their father lures them to Yemen to enjoy a holiday and to visit family members. But after arriving in Yemen, the girls are told they are married by now and disappear into an inaccessible area in the mountains. It takes several years before their mother succeeds in locating them again. (See: Miriam Ali, *Without Mercy*.)

On top of the personal suffering for the girls and their involuntarily started families, it is striking how in both the British and the Yemeni legal systems, men are able to take advantage of their dual nationality, while the girls by the same two legal systems are forsaken. The girls are involuntarily made to be Yemeni nationals and held incommunicado. Father Muhsen collects the dowry of his daughters, he has gambling debts. This act is a violation in both countries involved, but no one holds him accountable. ('There is no proof'.) In fact he sells his daughters as trafficked women. Afterwards, he and the new fathers-in-law continue to travel back and forth between England and Yemen undisturbed. The UK authorities refrained from taken steps to retrieve the misguided under aged girls. Because the case of their involuntary marriages became 'a Yemeni family matter' in which the British government cannot get involved.

Meanwhile, father Muhsen remarries a Yemeni wife and has lived with his new family back in England ever since.

Source: Zana Muhsen, *Sold: a story of modern-day slavery.*

5.9 Recent developments

Guardianship of the mother

As a society changes, its legislation changes alongside. Some life stories highlight modern movements in the tight regulations. An example is the story of Malika Kaddour. She gets the cooperation of the Syrian courts when she applies for custody of her abducted children.

Malika Kaddour is born as an Algerian Muslim, who grows up in the Netherlands. In 1988 she meets Hamid, a ' Muslim asylum seeker from Lebanon " who has lived in the Netherlands for eleven years. They start a relationship, although they do not get married. Her parents object as they do not trust Hamid. Initially, Hamid shows himself as a loving and caring partner, but not for long. The relationship deteriorates. Hamid is unpredictable, cannot hold on to a job and mistreats her. Malika's father often has to help out financially. Two daughters are born. But after seven years they break up. The children stay with Malika, while Hamid gets visiting rights. Hamid continues to stalk her. In 1999, when the children are four and nine years, Hamid abducts them to Syria. By then it is discovered that he is not a Lebanese Muslim, but a Syrian Christian. Malika travels to Syria and mobilizes all help she can get, lawyers, journalists, friends, and the Dutch embassy in Damascus, to get her children back.

Initially, she is advised not to travel to Syria by herself, she could be arrested. But that danger she brushes aside. She finds out that her girls commute between the sister, the mother and another relative of their father. The family frightens the girls by saying that the lady from the Dutch embassy, who tries to visit them, will put them in an orphanage.

However, the judges in Syria are well-disposed to Malika, as Hamid has lied about his religion. He has deceived a Muslim woman. Moreover, he is arrested for evading military service. The judge assigns the children to Malika, provided she raises them in Syria. She accepts this agreement. But fortunately an opportunity arises to slip through the border into Lebanon. On the other side helpers stand ready to escort mother and daughters to the airport. After more than a year the three of them are back in the Netherlands, back home.

Source: Malika Kaddour, *Stolen daughters*. Amsterdam: Arena 2003

From Tunisia similar stories are heard. In Tunisia, Loudy Nijhof and Esma Abdulhamid win a custody lawsuit of their children, who were taken from them by their fathers. Loudy can take her son back to the Netherlands, Esma her three children to Germany. It was not an easy process for either of them, and required a lot of money and patience.

The Dutch woman Loudy Nijhof meets Hamza on holiday in Tunisia in 1992. They start a relationship, later that year Hamza moves to the Netherlands. They do not marry, but settle for a civil registration, which authorizes Hamza's residence permit. But the relationship has serious ups and downs; Hamza is unpredictable and mistreats Loudy. As his Tunisian family often calls with all kinds of claims, the couple travels to Tunis several times. When their son Alaya is born in 1997, their relationship has already deteriorated. In 2000, Hamza travels with their son to Tunisia, with Loudy's permission. Without telling her, he has the child circumcised. Hamza returns without his son, but with another (Dutch) girlfriend. Loudy presses charges on her ex, who then contributes to the return of Alya. In September 2004 Hamza and Loudy get joint legal custody of their son. But later that year, Hamza again takes the boy with him to Tunisia, for both of them to stay. Loudy again presses charges, and when Hamza sometime later travels to The Netherlands, he is arrested at Amsterdam Airport for child abduction.

Loudy quickly finds out that Hamza's family, with whom she was on good terms, now totally oppose her. Her son stays with his Tunisian grandmother. A Tunisian court decides that the child is Tunisian, but that the mother is entitled to visitation rights. Loudy undertakes several trips to Tunisia to see her son. The Tunisian family is angry about the arrest of Hamza and blames Loudy. Hamza often calls from the Dutch prison with his family and remains angry with Loudy. On his orders, the family does everything possible to frustrate her visitation rights. If Loudy makes an appointment to visit, Alaya is 'still in school', or 'just somewhere else" or ''will be right there.'

When the Dutch consul in Tunisia wants to visit Alaya, he turns hysterical with fear and hides. Later is found out that Alaya was made to believe that the consul lady would come to abduct or poison him.

Loudy moves heaven and earth to take Alaya back home. Meanwhile, in Holland, Hamza appears in court. It is proved that he commissioned the kidnapping and instructed his family not to let Loudy see the child.

Early in 2006 the Dutch TV program NOVA broadcasts a report on Loudy's story. The report leads to much controversy, also in Tunisia. In April 2006, after nerve-racking months, the Tunisian courts decide on her behalf and she may take her son home.

Source: Loudy Nijhof, *Mama comes to fetch you*, Dordrecht The Free Press 2010

Somewhat similar is the story of Esma Abdelhamid.

The Tunisian woman Esma Abdel Hamid, born in 1960, is married off to a Tunisian guest worker in Germany in 1979. The two of them had never met before. The couple settles in Hamburg. It is a marriage without affection or appreciation. Husband Abdullah belittles and mistreats Esma and constrains her freedom. Every year they spend the summer with relatives in Tunisia. Esma then keeps up appearances of a happy and good life. Three children are born.

In the summer period of 1990 Abdullah steals Esma's passport and leaves her with their youngest child, a daughter, in Tunisia.

But in the spring of 1991 Esma succeeds in acquiring a new passport and a visa for Germany, and pays an unexpected visit to her marital home, where Abdullah now lives with a new girlfriend. But Esma is not to be sent away anymore.

Abdullah makes a move to reconcile with her. But after doing so, he sends the other two children to Tunis, fetches his daughter from the grandparents and brings the three of them to an uncle who lives far away in the Tunisian countryside. He divorces Esma, but claims to others that it is she who left him.

Back in Tunisia, Esma barely manages to make use of her visiting rights, as her ex in-laws do everything they can to alienate her children from her, using all the tricks of malicious abuse to an ex-spouse.

With the help of her own parents, Esma overcomes her plight. She applies for custody of her children at the Tunisian court. She claims that the father does not look after his children and they have no good life at their uncle's either. Pending the procedure Esma goes back to Germany, because she must be able to care for them to get custody. In a German shelter house for women Esma learns the German language and gets support on how to build up an independent life. In 1993 the Tunisian court grants her custody. A few months later the children return to Hamburg. The problems are not over yet as the children feel estranged, not only from their mother but also from Germany. Nevertheless, she manages to build a new family life.

Source: Esma Abdelhamid, *I fought for my children*. Amsterdam: Arena 2009

In all three cases described here, the father did not look after his children himself after abducting them, but placed them under the care of family members with the intention of blocking their contact with their mother.

Studies on family law are soon obsolete. So, already by the time of printing of this book there are new developments. It is recommended to be aware of the latest news. But is equally important realizing that a change in rules not automatically aligns with a change in mentality. One does not automatically get what one is entitled to.

The American magazine Newsweek reports a catching up for women in education and economics. The female half of the world is better equipped to cope with economic recessions than the male one. In developing countries, that trend is already visible. Women take their place in the labor market and often are more successful than men.

Newsweek July 12, 2010. Women & Leadership, pp 37-45.

UN Convention of Women

In 1979 the General Assembly of the United Nations human rights adopted the treaty for women's rights. Sections 15 and 16 deal with family law: men and women are entitled equal rights. Almost all UN member states have signed the treaty. But the countries with patriarchal family legislation made reservations on these two articles, as being inconsistent with their national legislations. So, there is still work to do for the international women's and human rights movement.

The Convention of The Hague

In 1980 in convention against child abduction was drawn up in The Hague, Netherlands. It is called the Convention of The Hague. The convention also contains articles which state that a child of a certain age - usually twelve years - must determine him/herself with which parent in which country he / she wants to live. The countries where the father has more parental authority than the mother, did not endorse this child abduction treaty.

Loudy Nijhof also appealed to the UN Convention on the Rights of the Child, as Tunisia has signed the Convention in March 2004.

Article 11 reads: The countries that have signed the Convention commit themselves to actively combat illicit transfer of children abroad. The interpretation of this article has not been elaborated; this is different in every country. Again, from the standpoint of universal human rights there still is much to be achieved.

6 Advice for parents of the bride

6.1 Introduction

This chapter addresses the parents and other relatives of the export bride with suggestions on how to support the bride-to-be.

The life stories present very little information about the opinion of the parents. The authors don't give an insight into whether their parents support or oppose their daughter's marriage plans. On the other hand, if their daughter meets marital problems, the parents do not let her down, but try to help her.

Since parents in the Western world only play a minor role in the marital choices of their children, parents are hardly involved. On the contrary, in general, parents leave their sons and daughters complete freedom in their choice of partners, even if the daughter chooses a foreigner from a patriarchal culture as her bridegroom.

A bride is precious

In countries with other kinds of family relationships things go a different way. Especially in cultures where men and women do not enjoy equal gender rights and where in family life the husband is the boss. In such cultures, the loving parents of daughters see it as their duty to lead their child into marriage in a strong position. They 'sell her at as high a price as possible', so to speak. She should be a wealthy and respectable bride. In countries with an Islamic culture such as Morocco and Egypt, the bride's marriage guardian will negotiate firmly with the marriage guardian of the other party. In a worst case scenario, like the consequences of divorce, widowhood, bankruptcy, or serious illness of the breadwinner, she should not be left without means of her own. Western parents do not think about these issues, as coping with financial disaster is regulated in their own national laws and often solved outside the family. But the influence of a Western welfare state stops at the border. A bride, who neither contributes nor negotiates, is obtained for 'free' and is "valueless', not precious.

Parental involvement

We now directly address the parents. Being a parent of a future bride, you have more influence in the arrangements than you imagine. You can contribute to a proper entry of your daughter into her new life. Failing to do so is letting your daughter down in the culture of her in-laws. In the life stories, these points come up.

The German woman Heike Wagner marries in 1959 the Egyptian Ahmed at twenty years of age. She meets him during his studies in Cologne. He presses her to marry quickly, from reasons of decency. After the birth of their son the family leaves for Egypt. They move in with the patriarchal family. It turns out that Ahmed's stories about his successful study in Germany are unfounded. Due to inadequate performance, his father instructed him to come back and puts him to work in the family business. Heike also finds out that there was already a bride arranged for him. Ahmed has jilted her to marry Heike.

Ahmed changes his behavior. In Germany he was an attentive husband who often spent time with her. In Egypt, he retreats into the world of men, hardly talks to her and commands her in bed. When he beats her up, the other married women of the family regard her as one of them. Wives should be humble (sabr). Ahmed develops a malicious pleasure in controlling Heike. Her passport goes in the safe; he does not allow her to travel. For Heike his behavior is ambiguous: he belittles her, calls her names, hardly talks to her, scolds her as a whore, but to others he speaks highly of her. So, the family is made believe he loves her.

When Heike's mother comes for a family visit to Egypt, Heike's in-laws greet her warmly. Heike hides her unfortunate position from her mother.

Ahmed's father wishes Heike to convert to Islam. A non-Muslim wife cannot inherit from her husband or in-laws. He assumes she comes from a simple poor family, as she did not contribute anything in her marriage. That means poverty in later life. Moreover, being not a Muslim, she will go to hell after her death. Her caring father-in-law wants to spare her from such a fate.

After three years she travels with Ahmed to Germany. He refuses to take their son along. In Germany Heike flies from him and divorces. She only sees her son again years later, when he is of age and visits her in Germany. After Ahmed's death she can travel to Egypt to see her son and grandchildren without problems, as Ahmed never recognized the divorce in Germany.

Source: Heike Wagner, *Caught in the country of my beloved.* New York: Tirion 2000

Often, a daughter feels ill-disposed about involvement of her parents. She says she can take care of her own affairs. She sees each remark as a criticism about her choice of partner. In that case, tell her you want to get involved in the preparations of her wedding.To a request like this, your daughter will respond. If so, under the pretext of 'wedding arrangements' you have a valid reason to contact the future bridegroom and in-laws, not only to discuss the ingredients of the wedding cake, but also to find out the opinion of the future family-in-law about pre-nuptial agreements for their foreign, exotic daughter-in-law.

6.2 Negotiations

How are parents able to prepare their daughter for the important step in her life? The core advice for parents, especially for the father, is: imagine yourself in the position of the parents of a bride from the culture of the future son-in-law. What do these parents do, and more specifically, what is father's responsibility in preparing his daughter for her marriage? Check whether a sister or other female relative of the future son-in-law married recently and find out what the parents of that bride have arranged. Or ask the groom-to-be about his opinion of a proper marriage arrangement for his own sister or other close member of the family. Are long-time married couples still content with the arrangements made at their own wedding? Compare the answers you get with the treatment your own daughter may expect.

Marriage guardian

You might find out that the father acts as his daughter's marriage guardian. His task is to negotiate the marriage contract with the groom's family. From the father of the bride's point of view, the main purpose of such a contract is to protect the daughter against the many pitfalls she might encounter during married life. There are quite a few items in the contract a Western bride never would think of. Does she want to continue to work in her own profession? Does she want to visit her own relatives often, or once in a while? Note everything down. Does she wish to use her right to care for her own children if she divorces or becomes a widow? Full custody rights would be even better, is this possible? It often is a shock to find out too late that these matters concerning wife's rights are not obvious. On the other hand, matters which are self-evident in the groom's culture are not mentioned in marriage contracts. Community of property within a marital union is often an unknown phenomenon. This means that the assets which each spouse brings in or acquires during marriage, do not belong to the other one. Nevertheless, it is wise for the wife to insist on a bank account of her own.

Another idea is to buy real estate in her name in her home country. This could be a simple summer cottage, or part of a building. Do stipulate she can visit to stay there on a regular basis and do reserve funds for this purpose. A piece of private property, even small or only in name, will contribute to her position and independence. Moreover, in times of emergency, the front door of such a 'home' can be her 'backdoor'.

A jewel among the life histories is the book *Boundless love* by the anthropologist Hanneke Rozema. While living in Egypt, she interviews a number of Western women who are currently married, divorced or widowed. All the ups & downs of the married lives of these women are discussed. It is an amazing fact that the positive response to the groom's marriage proposal often is taken at breakneck speed. This means a start for disaster, according to the author. But to get to know each other well is only possible within the boundaries of a marriage. The Egyptian wedding ceremony takes place in a public notary office of a dusty and austere style. The couple signs some papers which the foreign bride does not understand. The official thinks it strange and sad that the young European woman does so by herself. "Who is representing you?"

Usually, the foreign brides make little or insufficient use of information and good advice available from the side of her embassy or other sources. Later on, they will say they did not see the importance at that moment. The romantic pink cloud veiled the view. But the experiences of widows and divorced women do not lie. Those who have contributed nothing beforehand and don't have any income of their own are literally empty-handed after a divorce. If they want to keep in touch with their children they have to remain in Egypt, but get no alimony. This also is the fate of widows, when a male relative of the deceased spouse not only cares for her and her children, but strictly controls them at the same time.

Rozema devotes an informative chapter to facts and tips for brides and their families and friends. A positive attitude and active involvement of the parents of the bride are very important. Proper preparations will contribute to the success of the marriage and should certainly not be seen as point of distrust of the future son-in-law.

Source: Hanneke Rozema, *Boundless love.* Amsterdam: Bulaaq 2005

As seen in a previous chapter, Western fathers in the nineteenth and early twentieth century had an important say at the wedding of their (adult) children. This paternal role changed and diminished in the course of time. But as a present-day father you should not forget that for your grandfather and great grandfather negotiations as marriage guardians were a regular part of the paternal tasks. Then it sounds less strange that, although several generations later, such a role is still very much alive in other countries.

It certainly makes a favorable impression on the parents of the groom if the bride's parents want to meet them beforehand. It is possible to correspond by e-mail or make telephone calls (skype!), or, maybe, to visit the future country of their daughter in person. It is important to see what the future environment of their daughter looks like.

In the negotiating period, see to it that the recorded points are legal and can be enforced in court. Informal arrangements, without the possibility of enforcement, are valueless. Remember that a contract is required for protection against disasters in the long term. Should she ever have to rely on her own resources, she must be able to do so. That is the starting point.

A foreign adult woman is allowed to represent herself. Therefore, no independent young Western woman will contemplate asking her parents (father, or brother) to fulfill the role as her marriage guardian. But by signing a marriage contract herself in an unknown foreign language, the bride is very vulnerable without being aware of it. Many women find this out too late.

Jacqueline Gillespie is only seventeen years old when she answers 'yes' to a question and puts a signature somewhere, after which she finds out she is married according to Islamic law! She says she did not know she was signing a marriage contract. But, nevertheless, the commitment is sealed, although, according to the same Islamic laws, a minor cannot sign such a contract.

Source: Jacqueline Gillespie, *Yasmin*. Baarn: Tirion 1998

Fathers are often better able to plan for the long term than a daughter in love.

Also remember that a marriage means a commitment for two family groups, who have a shared interest in a proper arrangement. A strange, foreign bride is a fremdkörper, a "foreign body" without ties and she therefore embodies a threat to the stability of the family clan.

6.3 Patriarchal son-in-law

The following advice is applicable for the period that the couple is married. Put yourself in this period in the position of parents of a married daughter in a patriarchal culture. Modern Western parents often like to support their married children with matters such as buying a house, investing in a business or an advance payment on an inheritance. Remember that it is unusual in the patriarchal family to do so for the married daughter. The material responsibility for the young couple is the concern of the husband and *his* family.

Gifts

So, in case you want to support your daughter financially, make sure that *she* is entitled to this support and it remains under her control. As already mentioned, it's good to allow her to possess a house or part of it in her home country and put a stipulation in the marriage contract that she can stay there at times to see her family, for example every Christmas or summer holiday. If there is also a fund with travel money available, then lack of money cannot be used as an excuse by the husband in case he is unwilling to give permission for

his wife's family visit. Do stipulate travel permission for her
as well (which is not obvious), preferably together with her
children.

Should you arrange financial gifts otherwise, e.g. to donate
money to the couple or to invest in his family business, she
might end up with nothing if the marriage breaks up. *He
is legally entitled to keeps all assets for himself.* In the life
stories, we read about such problems.

Hanneke Rozema tells the story of a foreign bride in Egypt,
who for many years puts her own income and labor into her
husband's business. She does so for the sake of the welfare
of the family. But when her husband suddenly dies, she is not
entitled to what she considers her share of the business nor
any other inheritance. Everything, the inheritance and all the
money she invested in the business, is claimed by his brother.
This brother-in-law does not allow her to carry on with the
business by herself. On the contrary, he now is her and her
children's guardian. From now on, he decides how much
money she gets to live on and how her children are educated.
Could such a situation be prevented? What would an Egyptian
wife have done? Well, an Egyptian business-minded wife
would have put her money is his business as *a loan* to her
husband. The loan then is laid down by a lawyer in an official
document with clauses on interest and repayment. Had the
foreign wife done so, then the brother, who took over the role
as head of the family, would have had to act as stipulated in
the loan agreement.

Source: Hanneke Rozema, *Boundless love.* Amsterdam: Bulaaq 2005

Marital Problems

If there are marital problems, the daughter often hides this from her parents. She does not want them to worry. Usually, parents cannot interfere with marital problems of their children, but staying on speaking terms with his family can make a big difference. Try to prevent broken ties with your daughter. In case the relationship with her leaves much to be desired, then put the communication on hold on a temporary basis, but keep a line of contact open.

In 1988 the Dutch woman Janneke Schoonhoven meets Hisham from Syria on holiday on the Mediterranean Sea. She is 22, he is 34 years old. They marry within a year and settle in Groningen in the Netherlands. Janneke's parents are concerned about her choice of partner, but stand by her. They help Hisham to get settled in his new homeland.

After the wedding, Hisham changes his behavior. He is charming and tender with a lot of sex, but he also is demanding and bosses her about. Janneke hates his fickle behavior, but she is still in love and tries to adapt. Her parents continue to support the young couple financially with the purchase of a house and the rendering of various services.

Hisham wants no children, but when they do come - a son and a daughter - he plays a fatherly role. He learns Dutch, and finds a job as an interpreter for refugees. But at the same time he entertains all kinds of connections and relationships, about which Janneke is kept in the dark.

The couple visits the family in Syria for the first time when Janneke is pregnant. The family greets her warmly. However, she also observes that Hisham often quarrels with members of his family.

The fights in their relationship increase, according to Hisham it's always her fault. He calls her parents all sorts of names, even tells his mother-in-law she's a witch. The parents sever ties with Hisham, but when Janneke reconciles with him, they accept that.

The marriage breaks up. The two children are assigned to their mother while the father gets visitation rights. But the problems are far from over. Hisham stalks her, and alternates charming moments with irritation, like before. Janneke gets very nervous. Meanwhile, he finds a new girlfriend. Janneke also meets a new partner with whom she remarries. The children see their father regularly, as arranged. A week's holiday in France with their father and his girlfriend is no problem for Janneke as the girlfriend treats the children well. Although she realizes he can abduct the children, she does not think that will happen, as Hisham has his home, job and new relationships in the Netherlands. Moreover, he always indignantly denied ever doing such a thing. But then, in August 2004, father and children do not return after another holiday in France. Hisham takes his children to Syria.

The aftermath of the abduction has gotten extensive coverage in the Dutch press. Janneke travels to Syria several times, and contacts everybody she thinks can be of help, the Ministry of Foreign Affairs, the Dutch embassy in Damascus, lawyers, TV, the press, the House of Representatives.

Meanwhile, Hisham plays the holy innocent and tells his children that their mother does not want them back. *He* is the victim of this situation, he would gladly return to the Netherlands, but he is threatened (according to other sources he is the one who has threatened other people). He stands his grounds as a father, according to the Syrian family law. Janneke's visits to Damascus are chaotic and dramatic.

The children succeed in fleeing to the Dutch embassy after two years of residence in Syria. There they stay as refugees for over six months. Only after lengthy negotiations and under intense pressure does Hisham allow his children to travel back to the Netherlands. After an absence of nearly 2.5 years, they return to their mother escorted by the Dutch ambassador.

Source: Janneke Schoonhoven, *Do not touch my children. The story of the mother of Sara and Ammar.* Baarn: De Kern 2007

6.4 Divorce

It is not always clear how parents can support their daughter in a divorce procedure. It is a good thing to realize that in patriarchal societies, it is a disgrace for a man if his wife is the one who wants a divorce. If she insists, he must accept it, but then will do everything to thwart her, more so when there are children involved. If the foreign wife wants to return to her homeland with the children, he can stop this. The children belong to him, the father. She is either allowed to leave on her own, or he sends her away. Many biographies deal with nasty divorces with unhappy aftermaths.

Tact

It is therefore important to use a lot of tact and discretion. It is wise for the parents of the divorcing wife not to speak badly about the son-in-law. An attitude of mourning works better: "How terrible it is that things are going this way. We would have loved if the developments were different. This is very sad." Indicate you cannot prevent the divorce, so do not insist on reconciliation, but keep your distance. Avoid aggravating your daughter's troubles. The adage that one catches more flies with molasses than with vinegar is applicable here.

If the divorce procedure takes place in her home country, it seems a natural thing for her to take the necessary initiatives. But it is wiser to leave these to the husband, even if he operates in a clumsy matter when dealing with the bureaucratic system than his wife. In his culture it is dishonorable when his wife lays down the law on him. Try to bend the course of events in such a way that it is he, not she, who initiates and controls the procedures. If the outcome is no blow on his 'honor', his ex-wife will meet more goodwill towards her wishes about the divorce settlement and visitation rights for the children.

Dishonor

Nevertheless, a stigma of disgrace sticks to the husband. Especially if it is clear that the divorce is (also) her wish. But when the break is inevitable, he starts towards reconciliation. Several writers mention they receive moving letters from their ex later on. He misses her so much and hardly can imagine that there really were serious conflicts. Or he knows this very well, but promises to improve his life. He will be the happiest man in the world if she comes back to him. New prospects bring a golden future.

Your daughter is in a dither. She remembers the highlights of the relationship, reviewed in his messages. She thinks of going back to him. If this happens, do keep in mind that his overtures do fit into the aftermath of coming to terms with his loss of honor. He must try to win her back. But it is an empty gesture. Should the ex-wife give in, things might make a turn for the better, but more often the restoration of good relations only is temporary. After a short period of time the situation is the same as before. If she does not comply with his courtship, the ex-husband's regret about the divorce immediately dies down and he resumes his old aggressive behavior.

In such circumstances, support from her side of her family will do a lot of good for the daughter in trouble.

7 Advice for the bride(-to-be)

7.1 Introduction

The authors of the life stories entered their intercultural relationships full of confidence in the future. Although many of them faced a disillusion, remarkably often they say not to regret the life enriching experience and take the trouble to write down their remarkable story. Life stories contain a rich source of information on do's and don'ts for young women with intercultural wedding plans. The stories provide answers to questions how to avoid and to cope with undesirable situations. What kind of support from your family you like best? In short, what is important to know in advance?

Information on legislation and consequences of a marriage contract should be compulsory reading for all couples who are about to marry. But this is even more important for international, intercultural couples. However, the life stories tell that many a future bride did not bother at all to get acquainted with formalities. Too late they found out that an investment in future knowledge not only helps in making the relationship successful, but is more humane and less costly than the pain and costs of failures as well.

7.2 Preparations

Now we focus directly on a (young) woman with intercultural wedding plans. The key advice to get prepared is to imagine yourself into the position of a bride from his family or his culture. What would such a bride settle for and why does she do so? Which preparations she thinks are necessary for a happy married life and protection against a possible worst case scenario which might befall her in the course of time?

Marriage Contract

Do not become a victim of good faith and ignorance. The practical aspects in a marriage contract are of great importance. In Western countries, the drafting of prenuptial agreements by a notary is possible, but only caters for material issues, like finances. Such a contract is not compulsory and is also still viewed with skepticism. «Do you not trust each other?" In patriarchal family law, to draw up a contract is legally required. So, if you imagine being a bride from his culture, ask yourself: what will that bride prefer and arrange if she should marry your groom? Or, what will your groom expect if his bride comes from his own culture? In case he breaks up an earlier marriage arrangement to wed his new foreign wife, find out which arrangements were made and broken. Are you blamed?

The contract-to-be contains a lot of items a Western bride never would think of. Do you want to continue to work, to practice your profession? Get it listed.

The wish for a yearly family visit to your home country is quite reasonable. Mention this point plus a saving for this purpose. If you become widowed or divorced, will you use your right to care for the children? Let your requirements be authorized by an official, his father or a notary of his country to make these enforceable. Requirements or wishes which are granted off the record (like: but my dear, anything you want, I'll give you. No need to include in the marriage contract), have no value. But, a sincere groom will inform you about your rights and obligations in due time. If he fails to do so, he neglects his duties regarding care for his future wife.

Also remember that a bride without a list of pre-nuptial demands is not appreciated as a modest woman, but rather as a stupid one. Make sure you know about the proper procedures.

In the Islamic sharia legal system no woman gets married without the active involvement of her parents. They must authorize the marriage contract, the dowry she gets, the bride price she is entitled to, and negotiate about her demands and wishes. In Western countries this course of affairs is a thing of the past. Still, if your fiancé respects his own cultural rules, he should be suspicious if you say you do not need parental consent. He should insist on the blessing of your parents about your relationship with him. It adorns him if he wants to know their opinion about him, as he takes over the responsibility for your welfare from them.

This is not a new idea. Already much earlier, the suggestion was put forward that "it is desirable in case of a marriage to a Muslim man to make a notaries act containing a clause of monogamy and a fixed monthly allowance for the woman, if possibly supplemented with other elements of the Islamic matrimonial law. But it is doubtful whether the bride wants to make use of this possibility while it is not clarified either is such an act is valid abroad (in the Muslim man's country)."

In any case, it is advised is to find a lawyer, who specializes in international family law.

Embassy

Before leaving for your new country, write down the data from the embassy or consulate of your home country. Phone numbers, email addresses, websites, opening hours, whatever is applicable. These data are available on the Internet. Get yourself registered upon arrival. If necessary, the authorities can reach you. In countries with many foreign brides, embassies have useful information available about the local marriage laws and the possible pitfalls. Make use of that information.

Knowledge migrant

If you have a profession you can carry on in your new country, find out whether you can enter the country as a migrant with special skills. Do so before departure. A high skilled migrant has different, and better, perspectives than a 'regular' marriage migrant. An example is Mirjam van Roode, who was able to find an interesting job in Kenya before settling there. So, she could combine the positions of a skilled professional and of an import bride.

Marital Life

How do you imagine the daily routine in your marriage life? Every night on the couch, to enjoy together the favorite soap program on TV? This is not very likely to happen. Observe how young couples, comparable to yours, live their lives. It is quite possible that your husband after the wedding behaves like his married brothers and friends and seeks the company of other men. In many mixed marriages, the daily life looks like a 'Janus household" in which the partners have separate plans for the day, separate friends and separate plans for the future. It is unusual that men and women lead a social life in conjugal togetherness. Ask yourself whether you can live with this reality.

Elderly

You have the intention to grow old together and enjoy a comfortable old age? Observe at a family visit to the husband-to-be's family how older couples live. Ask yourself whether that image is up to your expectations. If not, your future spouse will probably say that he has a very different lifestyle in mind. But you might expect that he will fall back on the examples of his youth. But how do you find out?

Did your husband grow up in a polygamous family? Is his father a nice person or a family tyrant? Are there men in the family, who are serially monogamous or polygamous? In such a case, do realize that this is the image of family life in which he was raised. Marianne Alireza and Tehmina Durrani did experience these marital situations.

Marianne Alireza's Saudi father-in-law was polygamous. Her husband Ali also takes a second wife, but not before divorcing Marianne. However, Ali's brother Muhammad does take his second wife into his household with his first wife. Although his first wife objects to this co-wife, she has no means to go against her husband's wish.

Marianne also gives a vivid description of the marriage of a male friend, who has three wives. These three ladies get along together like sisters. One day they invite Marianne to go fishing. The four ladies cast together their fishing lines.

Source: Marianne Alireza, *At the drop of a veil.* Boston: Houghton Mifflin 1971

The Pakistani woman Tehmina Durrani is the sixth wife of Mustafa. She describes him as a 'feudal lord', a tyrant who demands absolute obedience from his wife (and ex-wives) and children. After his sixth divorce, this time from Tehmina, Mustafa remarries soon again.

Source: Tehmina Durrani, *Tears of humiliation. The horrors of my marriage with 'the Lion of Punjab'.* Amsterdam: Sijthoff Luiting 1994

Be informed about old age services. Do not count on a pension from the state, but rely on your own bank account from the very start of your marriage.

7.3 Being Married

Contract

In Islamic patriarchal cultures there is no conjugal community of property, like the custom is in many Western countries. Each of the partners keeps the money and the goods which he/she brings in at the wedding. If a married woman earns money, it is hers and remains hers. A man is responsible to support his family with his income. A woman, who invests her earnings or savings in the business of the husband, 'donates' this money to her husband, unless there is a contract made about a loan from her to him. A contract with your husband for repayment of money which should benefit the whole family sounds very strange to foreign ears. But this is customary, as his business is no common conjugal property. Look at whether such contracts do exist with his family or his business friends.

Different behavior

Western women, who step into an intercultural marriage, often mention that their husbands change their attitude after the wedding. Once married, a husband behaves less respectful. If he wants something, he doesn't just request so, but commands. In the courtship period this did not happen.

The Western wife wonders why he acts like that. Do the wives of his brothers and friends have similar experiences? Why, does he have to show who is boss? How do other wives think about this and how do they respond?

Children

Wait with getting children for at least three years. If the marriage breaks up after a short time because it was just a 'passport marriage' for the husband, the damage is limited. Pamela Green was not that lucky.

The British woman Pamela Green meets the Egyptian Abdel-Salem in England. They marry in Egypt in January 1979. Neither her family nor her in-laws support this marriage. The stories told by her husband about his background prove to be false, but nobody took the trouble to check these beforehand. Pamela helps her husband to get a residence permit in England. At a later date she makes "false statements" to assist the brother of Abdel-Salem to obtain a residence permit as well. Three children are born in England. Already before the birth of the third baby the marriage falls in a downswing. As soon as Abdel-Salem and his brother possess their residence permit, they don't need Pamela not any more. She is even abused by them. A divorce follows.

The Egyptian ex-husband and his mates in England act very cunning to gain the best of both worlds. Their English brides think they have a 'love marriage', but the men just use their wives for their own purposes, being the acquisition of two nationalities with the associated benefits. They leave their wives and children on the moment it suits them. Pamela is honest about her own naïveté in this regard. But then it is too late.

Source: Pamela Green, *Dear Children: a mother looking for in Egypt to her three abducted children.* Amsterdam: Forum 1995

Own passport

Make sure you always keep your own passport with you. Keep copies in a safe place and leave one on a familiar address, for example in the computer file of family or friends in your home country. Should you lose it or it is taken by the in-laws "for safety, it is a security", then it is easier to report a loss and file for a new one. As an additional security, besides a passport, an identity card can be useful.

Embassy

Get yourself registered at the embassy of your homeland. Attend events such as national day celebrations, preferably together with your husband.

Peer support

If your new country has 'foreign wives'-clubs; sign on and take part in the activities. There you meet other foreign wives, often from several nationalities, who befriend and support each other. If you happen to live in a country with many expats, then often you find thriving self-help organizations of 'expat wives' as well. To these organizations you can offer a useful contribution. Being part of the country, you know more about its peculiarities. Should your husband objects to your contacts with these other foreign women, he deprives you. It is unreasonably to demand you to lead a life, which isolates you from your own culture and friends.

7.4 Divorce

Male Rights

A man from a country with a patriarchal family law always retains his patriarchal rights in his home country, even if he emigrates to another country to get married. In case of a trip to his family in his country, his wife and children are subjected to his family laws during their stay over there. The foreign spouse often is ignorant about her change in status. The husband however, is not and does know he can decide whether he forces her to stay with him, or send her away as an unwanted alien. Among others, Betty Mahmoody in Iran, Elisabeth Stahlschmidt in Egypt, and Ilse Achilles in Pakistan had to face these, for them unwelcome, decisions.

Children

If your marriage ends in a divorce in which the (Dutch, or other Western) judge grants custody of the children to you, the mother, most probably the same judge will grant visitation rights to the father, even if you have objections. The father can abuse that right and abduct the children to his home country.

Once there, any judge will decide according to the wish the Muslim father, even if the father's demands are unreasonable or if he frustrates the contact with you as their mother. This problem is the main theme in many biographies.

Ask in advance whether or not you can claim custody, visitation rights, care rights and put those claims in writing. Also ask if those claims are valid should your husband fall seriously ill, incapacitated or dies. What are your parental rights in such circumstances?

Family Contacts

Keep good contact with your own family. In case of marital problems and divorce, you can often no longer rely on support from his family, even if you had a good relationship with your in-laws. The husband's family will stand by their own son or brother, even if they disagree with him. If they interfere at all, it is usually about insistence on reconciliation. Reconciliation from your side, that is. As marital problems are usually blamed on the wife, therefore the solution is placed with her as well. Many writers have experience with this attitude.

If you feel on your own, do not hesitate to accept help offered by others. It's good to have a back door. The front door of parents or friends might be that back door in times of distress.

The Dutch Jewish woman Sara emigrates to Israel. There she marries a Jewish man of Iraqi descent. In Sara's marriage, there are major cultural differences. Sara is a modern woman and a seasoned traveler; her husband is narrow-minded, macho, and dominant. The family of the groom thinks favorably about his marriage to a European wife, for status reasons. But, already after a few years and two children the relationship gets sour and Sara wants a divorce. The divorce is a war of attrition. In the final outcome Sara is left penniless (the ex-husband evades his alimony obligation) and more or less imprisoned in Israel. For the two small sons, who are assigned to her, her ex-husband has applied for and received a travel ban (a request for a travel ban on Sara is not granted, because she kept her Dutch passport). Should she take the kids abroad, she commits a crime, kidnapping.

The book describes the obscure bureaucracy of the country and the old-fashioned patriarchal family law. A woman, who applies for divorce harms the social status and honor of her man by doing so. Israel has organized interest groups for men's rights, which is an important social topic. 'Fatherhood robbery' is a serious allegation in Israeli divorce proceedings. Sara is not spared in this respect. The law offers inadequate protection to women, even less so to a foreign divorced mother. But Israeli friends from all sides come to the rescue. So, fortunately Sara not only counts on support of her family in the Netherlands, but can also rely on neighbors and peers in Israel.

Source: Rachel Levy, *Israel on an ordinary weekday.* Amsterdam: Contact, 2008.

7.5 Antenna

It is impossible to acquire a total picture of all the consequences of an intercultural marriage. However, it is possible to develop an antenna to identify, understand and appreciate strange situations. An intercultural relationship is more encumbered, but also much more challenged than a 'normal' relationship. Successful intercultural couples develop 'multiple cultural competences'.

7.6 Alarm Bells

If a relationship heads into the wrong way, there are advance warning signs. Do recognize these signals and act accordingly. Love does not conquer everything. The alarm bell rings in the following situations.

Violence

At the first sign of violence. Violence can take different forms.

Verbal abuse, such as snubbing, calling or shouting. This can happen unexpectedly for no obvious reason. You are scared. Perhaps you think you have to make amends for something, but without any idea what you did wrong. But such a reaction is counterproductive; because it means that for him a strategy of wickedness pays off. So, even if he makes excuses later on, you can expect this behavior to continue. Apologies afterwards often are not reliable. Should he have a good reason to be angry, even then verbal violence is not acceptable.

Sexual violence, enforcing actions that you do not want, never is acceptable in any culture. Sexual violence against women is a war crime, even in a marriage.

Physical violence and intimidation, that is never acceptable.

'Social' violence, which means that you will be thwarted when you want to see you own friends or communicate with your own family.

The enforcement of an 'I do' after a very short time. "You must decide now or never." In such a case, choose for the latter option.

Disrespectful behavior

Your (future) husband treats the women in his family disrespectful and rude.

He snaps off his sisters, commands, controls and belittles them. If he shows no respect for women, and his sisters (in-law) are afraid of him, keep in mind that he is capable to treat his own wife and daughters like this too.

If in family conflicts in which your husband is involved, his close relatives do support him unconditionally. Look carefully whether they do so because they agree with him or give this support blindly as this is just the way it should be. If the latter is the case, do not count on support from the husband's family for yourself in case of marital problems.

Vagueness

You are left in limbo about your status or position in your husband's country.

He leaves you ignorant or is vague about your rights as a married woman.

Uncertainty about your residence permit. Who is responsible for the application and how long is the permit valid?

Uncertainty about a possible work permit.

Uncertainty about recognition of your qualifications for jobs.

Uncertainty about the living situation. Your own home as newlyweds or live with the in-laws? For how long?

Partnership

Important questions about the conjugal partnership.

Obscurity about the family finances. Are you free to use the conjugal income as you like, or is his opinion: "I give you everything you need, and I decide what that is?"

He does not care or approve of you keeping your own bank account.

He manages to seize and to invest your income without your explicit consent.

He, not you, determines how you can spend your own money.

He does not make provisions to cope for 'old age' or problems such as illness or redundancy.

He does not support you in being self-determined, in being empowered.

Holiday romance

A romantic holiday is a wonderful experience, but highly insufficient as a basis for real life. So take enough distance, literally and figuratively, before you decide to continue the relationship. Your head in the (holiday) clouds may end up as a head in a noose. You are better off with good memories of a great vacation romance.

About a relationship which did not work out, the magazine *Linda* reports in 2010.

In Gambia, ugly ducklings suddenly catch the most beautiful men. And they have passionate sex. Fall in love with a black, proud warrior from Gambia. [...] There is nothing wrong with that, but there is only one thing you should remember: it is a holiday romance, nothing more or less. Holiday romances are fun because of the holiday. As a less cute ugly duckling in Gambia, you suddenly get attention from the most beautiful men. This has little to do with your personality, but a lot with your wallet.

Tineke of 55 years old meets Badou on holiday in Gambia, who is seventeen years younger. They fall in love, well, she falls in love. He turns out to be a passionate lover. "I said to myself: 'Tineke, you're 55 and not handsome, this man is using you!'" But I was blinded and only wanted more. I took him with me back to the Netherlands. But there my proud warrior changed in a shallow asylum seeker. It was a disaster. When I brought him back to the airport, I put five hundred U.S. dollars in his suitcase. I bought off my shame, and was relieved when the plane took off.

Source: Marleen Janssen, "Sand on my skin," *Linda,* August 2010, p. 64-69.

But a holiday can also lead to a thriving relationship.

Marguerite van Geldermalsen from New Zealand (her parents emigrated from the Netherlands) makes together with a friend a world tour in 1978. In Jordan's 'Rose Red' city of Petra, a prehistoric trading town situated on the ancient silk route, the girls like to spend a night in a cave dwelling. This can be arranged. Mohammed, who works as a guide and souvenir vendor in Petra, offers the ladies a suitable cave to stay overnight. The next day both tourists move on. But

Mohammed is touched. He follows the girls on their journey and invites Marguerite to accompany him to a wedding.

This event is the start of their romance. After some time Muhammad and Marguerite get married and live in a cave dwelling in Petra for many years. Three children are born. Marguerite finds a job as a nurse. A highlight is the visit of Queen Elizabeth to Jordan in 1984. Being a New Zealander, Marguerite is the only citizen of the British Empire in the wide area. Together with the Jordanian Queen Noor the British queen pays a visit to Marguerite and her family in Petra.

Eventually, the family leaves the cave dwellings for New Zealand. The marriage ends with the death of Mohammed in February 2002. The marriage of Marguerite and Muhammad, which started as a holiday romance, was very happy.

Source: Marguerite van Geldermalsen, *Married to a Bedouin, I lived in a cave* 2006

Politics

There may be political problems, or very cool relations between your country and that of your spouse. Such problems should stay outside the private and personal sphere, but nevertheless do effect family relationships.

You are treated with suspicion or hatred in his country, or your husband in your country.

You are hold accountable on political situations or decisions from your country about which you have no say whatsoever.

Your children may be the target of bullying.

An example of the latter is found in the 'Report of the Gulf War' of the Avalanche Foundation.

In the Netherlands, Dutch children of Arab fathers and Dutch mothers were bullied during the 1990-1991 Gulf War and after the attacks on the Twin Towers in New York on 11 September 2001. The children were of course completely innocent, so this was a troubling experience.

Pregnancy

Imagine the following situation. You're pregnant from your foreign boyfriend. You don't want to consider an abortion, but you don't want to marry him either. What to do now? Marry anyway, give birth and hope for the best? But is this a wise decision? You are at a loss. Well...

The best advice is to never to get married when you feel forced, but to postpone such a decision until you feel more relaxed and in control. It is better to return to your family and friends in your home country, and quietly await the birth. At the birth registration, list the child's mothers name and fill out 'father unknown'.

Remember that there is hardly a stigma on unmarried motherhood anymore. There are single women, who proudly bear the title BAM mother (Bewust Alleenstaande Moeder, Conscious Single Mother) as a nickname. 'Illegal' children no longer exist, as all children in your home country have the same rights.

In this way you keep full custody of your child as well as self-determination over your own life. Neither has your child the status of a (half) immigrant.

In case you decide later to continue the relationship with the father of your child, then paternity acknowledgment is still a possibility. Moreover, you are in a stronger position to negotiate.

Would you, however, while pregnant get married against your will, or you do no marry but you allow the father to register on the birth certificate, big troubles will arise if the relationship does not last after all. Quite a few women, who had doubts about the relationship but approved of the listing of the father on the birth certificate, do regret this bitterly.

The Dutch woman Loudy Nijhof describes how she allows her son's father, with whom she is not married, to register his name on the birth certificate. This was not required by law, but she wanted to make a kind gesture to him. A few years later, the father abducts the child to Tunisia. Only after much legal wrangling, Loudy manages to get her child back with exclusive custody rights.

7.7 Whether or not to marry

If problems do occur in the period shortly before the wedding, ask yourself if you really want to continue the relationship. You still can back off. That is not a pleasant decision to take; you need courage to do so, as you will raise a lot of criticism. Besides, your partner expresses regret for his rude behavior, if applicable, and promises to behave better. His family and perhaps also your family put pressure on you to reconsider that decision and to come back. The wedding date is set already, the guests are all invited and the wedding party is organized and paid for. But you should realize that all this insistence to reconsider has more to do with the dent that your fiancé's ego has got by you giving him the sack and with the irritation about having to cancel the beautiful festival while the expenses have already been made, and less with the affection that the partner-to-be and his family cherish for you. Think about your own long-term future; consider where your interests lie and wonder whether this is really what you want or what you've envisaged. Listen to your inner voice. Also remember that if you're not happy, your husband and any children will not be happy either...

If you encounter these doubts when you are already married, it is different. Are you just married and your husband already exhibits the behavior of a possessive husband who no longer needs to trouble himself to please his wife, as many women mention in their autobiography, then ask yourself whether you still can go back. Do you really want to start a family with this man? Remember that the longer you wait to step out a bad relationship, the harder it becomes. Even more so if there are children involved. A decision to move out never is a pleasant one. But if this is impossible, prepare yourself for a stressful marriage, which many difficulties to cope with. Perhaps for many years.

Because:
A smart bride looks far ahead.
A smart export bride looks even farther ahead.

Glossary

Autonomy	To decide autonomously on own life, self-determination
Bigamist	Married man with two partners, who do not know each other
Bride price	Payment from the groom to the bride
De facto	Actually, not according to the law
De jure	According to the law, lawful
Dating down	Relationship with a partner who has a lesser status
Dowry	Payment the bride receives from her own family when getting married
Emigrant	Person who (voluntarily) moves for another country to start a new life
Exotic	Preference for the foreign
Export bride	Woman who emigrates to marry
Expatriate (expat)	Employee who is temporary sent abroad
Gender	The whole of the social and cultural characteristics of a sex
Heterogamy	Married to partner from a different (social) background, a mixed marriage
Heterosexual	Married to partner of the opposite sex ('regular' marriage)
Homogamy	Married to partner of the same (social) background, unmixed marriage
Homosexual	Married to same-sex partner, gay marriage
Marriage migrant	Person who moves to another country to get married
Immigrant	Alien who enters a country

Import bride	Woman who enters a country to get married
Jus sanguinis	Right to citizenship by principle of hereditary
Jus soli	Right to citizenship by principle of territoriality, being born in that country
Knowledge migrant	Migrant with specific and valued knowledge
Matriarchy	Society or family or where the decision power rests with women (mothers); is rare
Matrilineal	Descent and succession determined along the female line
Migration	Moving to another country with the intention to settle there
Mixogamy	Degree of mix between spouses
Monogamous	Married to one partner
Nuclear family	Father, mother and children
Parda (purdah)	Custom to withdraw women from public life
Patriarchy	Society or family or where the decision power rests with men (fathers)
Patrilineal	Descent and succession determined along the male line
Polygamous	Married with more than one partner
Polyandry	Marriage of a women with more male partners; very rare
Polygyny	Marriage of a man with more female partners
Sharia	Islamic (family) law
Unilineal	Descent and succession determined along one line, either male or female
Self-determination	Autonomy, right to independently decide on one's own life

Self-reliance	Ability to decide over one's own life
Urfa marriage	Marriage commitment for a certain period

Literature

Abdelhamid, Esma & Marianne Moesle. 2009. *Löwenmutter*

Achilles, Ilse; Anya Butt & Miriam Butt. 1991. *6000 Kilometer Sehsucht*) Weert: M7P

Ali, Miriam & Wain, Jana. 1995.:*Without Mercy*

Alireza, Marianne. *At the Drop of a Veil. The true story of a California girl's years in an Arabian harem.* Houghton Mifflin Company, Boston 1971

Alireza, Marianne.1987. Women of Saudi Arabia. *National Geographic* 173, October 1987, pag. 422 - 453

Alleen of samen? Individu en gezin in de toekomst. 1997. *Nederlandse Gezinsraad en Centraal Bureau voor de Statistiek*

Alsanea, Rajaa Abdulla. 2008. *The girls of Riyadh*

Bhutto, Benazir.1988. *Daughter of the East. An Autobiography.* London: Hamish Hamilton Ltd.

Bokpê, Annette, 2003. *Der Kuss des Voodoo*, München 2002

Breger, Rosemary & Hill, Rosanna (ed.). 1998.*Cross-Cultural Marriage. Identity and Choice.* Oxford/New York

Braun, Marianne. 1992. *De Prijs van de Liefde. De eerste feministische golf, het huwelijksrecht en de vaderlandse geschiedenis.* Amsterdam: Het Spinhuis

Buba, Hans-Peter & Werner Ueltzen & Laszlo A. Vaskovics & Wolfgang Müller. Gemischt-nationale Ehen in der Bundesrepublik Deutschland. *Zeitschrift für Bevölkerungswissenschaft*, Jr. 10, 4/1984, S. 421 - 448

Buskens, L.P.H.M. 1998. *Islamitisch recht en familiebetrekkingen in Marokko.* Amsterdam: Bulaaq

Cigdem, Hülya. 2008. *De Importbruid.* Amsterdam: Arbeiderspers

Durieux, Evelyn. 1993. *Princesse aux pieds nus*, Paris 1992

Durrani, Tehmina & Hoffer, William. 1994. *My Feudal Lord*

Fei, Sandra. 1993. *Perdute*

Geldermalsen, Marguerite van. 2006. *Married to a Bedouin*

Gillespie, Jacqueline. 1998. *Yasmin. Once I was a Princess*

Goekoop-de Jong van Beek en Donk, Cécile. 1897. *Hilda van Suylenburg*. Amsterdam

Green, Pamela. 1995. *Dear Children*

Hofmann, Corinne.1999. *Die weiße Massai*

Hofmann, Corinne. 2003. Zurück aus Afrika

Hondius, Dienke. 1999. *Gemengde huwelijken, gemengde gevoelens. Aanvaarding en ontwijking van etnisch en religieus verschil sinds 1945.* Den Haag:

Hoog, C. De. 1982. *Partnerselectie bij huwelijkssluiting in Nederland.* Proefschrift Wageningen

Hoogendam, Jannie & Snoijink, Bob. 1995. *Littekens in mijn hart: ik verloor mijn kinderen.* Amsterdam: Luiting-Sijthoff

Jensen, Stine. 2005. *Turkse vlinders. Liefde tussen twee culturen.* Amsterdam: Prometheus

Jordens-Cotran, Mr L. Instemming met de verstoting, naturalisatie en de erkenning van Marokkaanse verstotingen: artikel 3 of 2 WCE? *Tijdschrift voor Familie & Jeugdrecht,* jaargang 17 augustus 1995 aflevering 7, pag. 146 t/m 151

Kaddour, Malika en Elzinga, Doris. 2001. *Gestolen dochters. Een Nederlandse moeder zoekt in Syrië naar haar ontvoerde kinderen.* Amsterdam: Arena

Khan, Dina. 1998. "Mixed Marriages in Islam: An Anthropological Perspective on Pakistan." *Journal of the Anthropological Society of Oxford,* volume XXIX, no. 1, pag. 5 –28.

Kleijwegt, Margalith. 2010. *Sofia. Verhaal van een verboden liefde.* Amsterdam

Stichting Lawine. *Verslag van de Golfoorlog.* 1991

Luyckx, Kristel, red. 2000. *Liefst een gewoon huwelijk? Creatie en conflict in levensverhalen van jonge migrantenvrouwen.* Leuven/Amersfoort: Acco

Mahmoody, Betty. 1987. *Not Without my Daughter*

Mahmoody, Betty. 1992. *For the Love of a Child*

Matlé, Andreas. 1998. *Sonay A.*

Mernessi, Fatima. 1985. *Achter de sluier (Sekse ideologie islam).* Amsterdam: Feministische Uitgeverij Sara

Muhsen, Zana & Crofts, Andrew. 1994. *Sold: a story of modern-day slavery.*

Muhsen, Zana & Crofts, Andrew.1999. *A Promise to Nadia*

Donya al-Nahi en Andrew Crofts, 2003. *Heroine of the Desert*

Donya al-Nahi en Eugene Costello, 2006. *No One Takes My Children*

Naranji, Corinne. 2004. *Bittere thee. De liefde tussen een Nederlandse en een Iraniër.* Amsterdam: Archipel

Njiké-Bergeret, Claude. 1998. *Ma passion africaine*

Nijhof, Loudy. 2010. *Mama komt je halen. Het verhaal van een ontvoering.* Vrije Dordtse Pers

Karima Ouchan, Fenneke Reysoo, 1999. *Nooit geschreven brief aan mijn vader.* Amsterdam: Bulaaq

Pascoe, Robin.1996. *Culture Shock! Succesful living abroad. A wife's guide.* Singapore/Kuala Lumpur: Times Books International

Perrier, Sophie. 2001. *De mannen van Nederland. Het onverbiddelijke oordeel van buitenlandse vrouwen.* Zutphen/ Apeldoorn: Plataan

Roode, Mirjam van. 2009. *De roep van de mapori. Een Nederlandse vrouw over haar leven en werk in Kenia.* Amsterdam: Artemis

Rozema, Hanneke. 2005. *Grenzeloze liefde. Westerse vrouwen over hun Arabisch-islamitische huwelijk.* Amsterdam

Sampayo, Sonia. 2009. *Princesa de África*

Sayyida Salme/Emily Ruete.1992. *An Arabian Princess between two Worlds; Memoirs, Letters Home, Sequels to the Memoirs, Syrian Customs and Usages. Edited with an introduction by E. van Donzel.* Leiden: E.J. Brill

Schipper, Mineke. 2010. *Trouw nooit een vrouw met grote voeten. Wereldwijsheid over vrouwen.* Houten-Antwerpen: Spectrum

Schoonhoven, Janneke met Roossink, Marlou. 2007. *Kom niet aan mijn kinderen. Het verhaal van de moeder van Sara en Ammar.* Baarn: De Kern

Speelman, Gé M. red. 1994. *Ik ben christen, mijn partner is moslim. De praktijk van interreligieuze huwelijken: verhalen en vragen.* Kampen

Speelman, Gé M. 2001. *Keeping Faith. Muslim-Christian Couples and Interreligous Dialoque.* Zoetermeer

Stahlschmidt, Elisabeth. 1998. *Auch ohne meine Kinder*

Trevane, Jacky. 2004. *Fatwa – Living with a Death Threat.* London: Hodder & Stoughton

Wagner, Heike. 2000. *Gefangen im geliebtem Land*

Zwaard, Joke van der. 2008. *Gelukzoekers. Vrouwelijke huwelijksmigranten in Nederland.* Amsterdam: Artemis & Co

Would you like to see your manuscript become a book?

If you are interested in becoming a PublishAmerica author, please submit your manuscript for possible publication to us at:

mybook@publishamerica.com

You may also mail in your manuscript to:

**PublishAmerica
PO Box 151
Frederick, MD 21705**

www.publishamerica.com

Lightning Source UK Ltd.
Milton Keynes UK
UKOW05f0820131013

218897UK00001B/3/P